THE GLOBAL HISTORY SERIES

Leften Stavrianos, *Northwestern University* /
General Editor

This series aims to present history in global perspective, going
beyond national or regional limitations, and dealing with overriding
trends and forces. The various collections of original materials span
the globe, range from prehistoric times to the present, and include
anthropology, economics, political science, and religion, as well as
history.

The editor of this volume, Creighton Gabel, has engaged in fieldwork in Central Africa. Author of numerous articles in American,
African, and European journals, he received his doctorate at Edin-
burgh. Dr. Gabel is Research Associate in the African Studies
Program and Associate Professor of Anthropology at Boston University.

Also in the Global History Series:

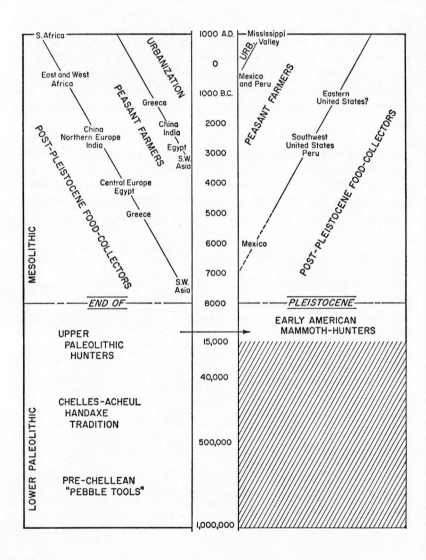

MAN BEFORE HISTORY

EDITED BY CREIGHTON GABEL

Prentice-Hall, Inc. / *Englewood Cliffs, N.J.*

PREFACE

The task of the prehistorian is to study and, insofar as possible, reconstruct human life as it was prior to the advent of written documents, whether these first appeared in given regions 5000 or 100 years ago. His means of doing so is through archaeological excavation, the only direct means of investigation available to him. What comes out of the ground is necessarily restricted to remnants of material culture—tools, weapons, pottery, sculpture, architecture, or anything else that may have physically survived the intervening centuries or millennia. Therefore, the interests of the prehistoric archaeologist are not in the identification of specific events or individuals but in the delineation of preliterate cultures. From the evidence, an attempt is made to define prehistoric behavior with respect to technology and economy, systems of belief, social and political structure, and aesthetics. Few if any such reconstructions can ever hope to be altogether complete or accurate because of the inherent limitations in basic facts, although it must be realized that there is a distinct difference between wild speculation and the well-reasoned inference which characterizes good archaeological work. Furthermore, the probability of any interpretation will be influenced by the amount and nature of material recovered, which may consist simply of stone tools scattered about in river gravels or include a multitude of artifacts and features from ruined towns or ceremonial centers. In his evaluations of prehistoric man, the archaeologist is frequently aided by scientific colleagues, especially geologists, botanists, and zoologists, who can help place cultural manifestations in proper temporal sequence as well as explain human activities and the environments in which they were carried on. Specialized chemical and physical techniques of analysis or dating are of immense value also.

The importance of prehistory to our understanding of man and his works scarcely can be overstated, for here are to be found not only the very origins of humanity but the sources from which developed all existing cultures and the foundations of literate civilizations. Most of our basic technology originating before the Industrial Revolution had its roots in the prehistoric past. Before any human thoughts or actions were put in writing, man had learned to domesticate plants and animals, to work metals, and to make ceramics and textiles. He had already invented the bow and arrow, the plow, the wheel, and the sailing ship. In some areas, mathematics and astronomy were being successfully pursued by men not yet literate, and some of their artistic, architectural, and engineering feats are among the wonders of the world. Stonehenge, Zimbabwe, Teotihuacan, and Altamira command the admiration of any modern visitor. Likewise, the formative threads of the world's religions can be traced back into dim antiquity, before ancient scholars had begun to write up their mythologies into a Bible or a Rig Veda. Many aspects of our social and political systems were formulated during prehistoric times as well, among people whom we can come to know only by digging through their settlements, cemeteries, tombs, shrines, and refuse heaps.

C.G.

CONTENTS

I / THE STUDY OF PREHISTORIC MAN

In the United States, a prehistoric archaeologist is normally trained as an anthropologist specializing in the field of archaeology. Anthropology, which can be most simply defined as "the study of man," consists of four major subdisciplines: ethnography and ethnology (the description and comparison of existing nonwestern cultures), linguistics (the description and comparison of unwritten languages), physical anthropology (the study of human evolution and biology), and archaeology (the description and comparison of extinct cultures). With a broad background in all these subjects, the archaeologist is better equipped to evaluate prehistoric cultural materials as a reflection of human activities and cultural change. None of this evidence can be utilized to the fullest extent without reference to living societies, and the archaeologist therefore constantly falls back on his knowledge of human behavior in recent times to help him interpret the behavior of earlier man.

The study of earliest man is concerned with biological as well as cultural development, and here the physical anthropologist specializing in human paleontology plays an extremely important role. For, although we assume, with good reason, that different cultures developed quite independently of biological factors during much of man's past, the initial evolutionary phases of human biology and culture are understandable only with reference to one another. In this sense, the bones and tools of our earliest ancestors are equally significant, and the physical anthropologist and archaeologist complement each other in their research. The physical anthropologist's examination of teeth and bones of later prehistoric levels furnishes a good deal of supplementary information on such things as nutrition, disease, mortality rates, and racial types.

The ethnologist's explanation of the processes of culture as seen in many different areas of the world provides the archaeologist with working theories that help him interpret in the most comprehensive fashion his sparse material evidence of cultural development and change.

Linguistics can be useful in the historical documentation of relationships between existing languages. Such kinships when established by linguists often furnish clues to prehistoric cultural connections that can be examined archaeologically. For example, both linguists and archaeologists have worked together to explain the origin of Indo-European languages in Eurasia and Bantu languages in sub-Saharan Africa.

Geologists, botanists, and zoologists also aid the archaeologist through their descriptions and analyses of soils, rock formations, animal bones, vetetation, and pollen found in or related to archaeological sites. This information is invaluable in determining the time at which a prehistoric culture flourished and the environmental conditions to which it was adjusted. Chemistry and physics contribute to the reconstruction of prehistoric cultures as well; radiocarbon processes help place objects in time and technical analyses of ceramic or metal composition may tell where objects were made or where the raw material was obtained for their manufacture. In modern archaeology, it is virtually impossible to write a report without reference to a half-dozen or more specialists in other fields.

The first step in field archaeology is recognition of prehistoric sites deserving excavation. Probably the question most often asked of archaeologists is, "How do you know where to dig?" It is usually not as difficult to determine this as the layman tends to think. Some archaeological sites, such as burial mounds of the midwestern United States, rock-built tombs of western Europe, or shell middens in coastal areas, disturb the natural topography enough for the practiced eye to identify them easily. In many instances, a prehistoric settlement is marked by substantial amounts of surface debris—arrowheads, potsherds, and so on—which give it away; in other cases, natural erosion, quarrying, or construction projects expose sites occupied by prehistoric man. Almost any cave or rock shelter of reasonable size is likely to have served some group of people, or even a series of them, as a convenient shelter; as a result, a disproportionate percentage of our information on early man in some locales comes from this kind of habitation, which can be readily identified. It is true that one may have difficulty locating sites in regions with a heavy vegetation cover and little erosion (such as tropical forests), but fortunately these conditions are relatively limited.

Even though some prehistoric settlements are not visible at ground level, they can be seen in aerial photographs either because the organic debris has promoted a change in their vegetation or because a bird's-eye view reveals the existence of walls, earthworks, or cultivation plots that are nearly obliterated. Any geometric pattern or other perfectly regular feature of the landscape visible from the air is likely to be of human origin. Little aerial photography is actually done for the express purpose of archaeological surveying, but there are large areas of many countries for which military or commercial air photos are available.

Finally, the archaeologist has learned through experience that certain geological deposits or natural areas (river terraces, shores of dried-up lakes, rock shelters) are worth exploring because the same or similar localities have been productive in the past. This methodical investigation has become more common in recent years and has tended to reduce the element of pure chance in discovering archaeological sites. With proton magnetometers or eletronic resistivity-measuring equipment, it is sometimes possible to locate subsurface disturbances, not otherwise detectable, that relate to prehistoric occupation.

When an area has been thoroughly surveyed archaeologically, even though not all the known sites have been completely excavated, it is feasible to make a study of prehistoric settlement patterns and derive some conclusions about the size and nature of occupation sites, their relationship to the environment, and the number of people who lived in them. The horizontal dimensions and depth of a site alone give the archaeologist a good notion of how many inhabitants it had and how permanent their settlement was. This approach to prehistoric demography greatly supplements the contents of sites by providing another form of insight into the activities of early man.

Archaeological fieldwork has often been compared to digging through a modern city dump or junkyard, where one finds all manner of refuse that some archaeologist of the future might use to describe our way of life. He would be able to identify changes in the style of automobiles, eating utensils, furniture, and perhaps even clothing, as he worked his way from top to bottom. All cultures change through time, although at different rates and in different ways. These changes in form and style (necessarily related primarily to material goods) often can be traced and dated within a single site on a stratigraphic basis. The "law of stratigraphy," adapted from geology, is the fundamental guiding principle of field archaeology; it simply means that younger material accumulates on top of older material. Barring certain kinds of disturbance, the lower layers, or strata, of a site will contain older artifacts or human remains than those of the upper levels. Sometimes the presence of foreign objects, like a German Volkswagen chassis in an American junkyard, allows what the archaeologist terms *cross-dating*. In this manner, two cultural traditions can be chronologically equated.

Other types of dating are also employed by the archaeologist. One common, though not usually very precise, method depends upon artifact *typology* and, in essence, is based on the proposition that cruder implements precede those of a more advanced design. What the archaeologist does with ceramics, projectile points, and hand axes, we might do with automobiles, demonstrating that Model-T's were built before Model-A's, which in turn were followed by later Ford cars. However, this concept must be applied with caution, for there are numerous exceptions. People could, and did, employ some types of tools or pottery for a long time without change or "made do" with very crude implements and utensils while their contemporaries elsewhere were producing much more sophisticated ones. The Volkswagen has been manufactured in the same style for over twenty-five years and is more comparable to an American car of the 1930's than to one being made now. Thus, a Volkswagen in a refuse heap might date to 1938 or 1964, although, just as in an archaeological site, one would probably find other evidence pointing in one direction or the other. By dividing large collections of material into typological categories, the specialist is able to study culture change and culture relationships within one site or area and to compare different sites or areas.

Another method, known as *seriation,* involves the manipulation of artifact types, such as pottery or arrowheads, on a statistical basis in order to date different sites relative to one another. The assumption behind this technique is that styles achieve a peak of popularity and then die out, usually over a considerable period of time. By computing the frequencies of various traits or types from several sites in a fairly restricted area (within which some cultural continuity is likely to have prevailed), it is possible to show when each was occupied relative to the others by the percentage of "older" and "newer" styles present.

Distribution of artifact types, in the sense that older ones are more widespread geographically than younger ones, may be indicative of their respective ages. For example, one could establish, without reference to other evidence, that stone arrowheads and spearheads are of greater antiquity than metal ones because they were much more widely distributed around the world. This is a useful hypothesis, but it is full of loopholes, since environmental barriers or cultural prejudices can easily disrupt a regular rate of symmetrical distribution.

Geology provides some valuable chronological aids by placing in proper time perspective natural deposits or events which have cultural associations. The study of river-terrace formation or of alternate raising and lowering of sea and land levels often help archaeologists date cultural assemblages found on river terraces or coasts. The succession of alternating glacial and interglacial periods of the Pleistocene Ice Age, as established by geologists, furnishes archaeology with a means of dating different phases of the Paleolithic, or Old Stone Age. In tropical regions, where less extreme climatic changes (mostly in rainfall) reflect the advances and retreats of continental ice sheets in the Northern Hemisphere, geologists' studies of soil and rock formations reflecting these changes have helped date prehistoric cultures. Also, by correlating these sequences from one area to another, there is some hope of simultaneously correlating the associated cultural stages.

Chemical alterations in certain materials provide another series of dating methods. Both the fossilization of bone and the patination of stone (its chemical change resulting from weathering) are indicative of some antiquity. Because these may proceed at different rates in different circumstances, they are of greatest utility in sorting out mixed deposits of bones or stone artifacts which pertain to various time periods. If, for example, some stone tools show more patination than others found with them, there is a good possibility that the former are the earlier. The relative age of prehistoric bones sometimes can be assessed through determination of chemical content, since some elements like fluorine gradually accumulate in the bone while it lies in the earth. Here again the rate varies with local conditions, such as the amount of ground water. For this reason, the method is most often applied to bones from a single deposit to see if all are of the same age. A number of fossil human remains have been tested in this manner to determine whether or not they were contemporary with the formation of the geological deposits in which they occurred. The answer is to be found in the amount of fluorine they contain compared with that in other bones from the same deposit. This is one of the means by which Piltdown man was exposed as a hoax.

Among the most precise methods of dating prehistoric cultures is *radiocarbon,* or carbon 14, *determinations.* This is a so-called absolute dating method because it gives results in calendar years rather than just demonstrating the approximate age relative to some other thing or event. The dates are established by measuring the amount of a radioactive isotope of carbon present in a specimen. This isotope accumulates during the lifetime of an organism and then disintegrates at a constant and predictable rate after death. The age of wood, charcoal, bone, shell, and other organic material is based upon the residual carbon 14 left in it. Although the isotope is theoretically always present, the amount eventually becomes too small to detect, and a specimen over 30,000-50,000 years old normally cannot be satisfactorily dated. There are further limitations as well. The process is expensive: it requires complex equipment and skilled technicians, and obviously one must have preserved organic matter to obtain a date at all. Furthermore, there is some concern and uncertainty regarding the contamination of samples, which results in dates being either too late or too early. It is quite clear, on the basis of inconsistencies within or between series of dates, that a sizable portion are incorrect. Nevertheless, the development of this process ranks as one of the greatest breakthroughs in archaeology during this century, for it is at present the only reliable means of independently dating and correlating prehistoric sites and cultures in different geographical areas. Prior to this, archaeologists were forced to rely upon purely typological or geological considerations.

Another type of dating by radioactivity has seen limited use recently: the *potassium-argon method*. This method covers a much longer time span and has been employed to date geological deposits a million or more years old which contain remains of early fossil man. However, the method is still somewhat suspect and requires further refinement.

The primary contribution of botany to chronological problems is *palynology*, or pollen analysis. The palynologist collects preserved pollens (which are highly resistant to destruction) from archaeological sites and identifies them under the microscope according to type and number so as to reconstruct prehistoric vegetation patterns that, in turn, can be tied in with climatic cycles. Pollen studies have been applied with particularly good effect in northwestern Europe, and they are being developed more and more in other areas.

Another botanical dating technique is *dendrochronology*, or tree-ring dating. This, like radiocarbon dating, gives dates in absolute years. It rests upon differences in tree growth from one year to another and from one climatic cycle to another as the result of variations in temperature and precipitation. On the assumption that one tree ring equals one year's growth, it has been possible to work back-ward two thousand years or so in time by making a continuous series of graphs of ring thicknesses from different trees. This is done by beginning with a tree cut at a known date and then comparing and splicing together individual graphs which overlap in time. In order to obtain dates, one must have wood or large charcoal samples in which the rings can still be discerned and matched against the master graph. There are limitations with respect to the tree species and the location in which the tree originally grew. Some kinds of trees do not display the requisite differential in growth, and no tree growing where it was able to tap a constant supply of water will show much difference in ring thicknesses. Furthermore, most areas have climatic variations that are either too severe or too slight to give the proper results. Because of this, the method has been used with great success only in southwestern United States.

Paleontologists contribute to dating through the identification of animal bones and the establishment of faunal sequences that mark off major epochs in the earth's history. From the types and numbers of extinct and living animals present the zoologist is able to deter-mine, roughly at least, the time period represented by a collection of bones from an archaeological site. Like the paleobotanist, the zoolo-gist also aids the archaeologist in reconstructing past environments and in distinguishing human dietary habits.

There are other dating methods, including *paleomagnetism, ob-sidian hydration, thermoluminescence,* and *solar-radiation periodic-ity curves,* but most are either unreliable or have yet to be fully adapted to practical use in archaeoloy. It must be emphasized that no single dating technique is foolproof in terms of accuracy or appli-cability. However, it is almost always possible to utilize more than one method, as well as to check the results with those obtained for similar material elsewhere.

Excavation procedures, although varying to some extent depend-ing on the local conditions and type of site, are based on fairly firm concepts of what one should look for and how it should be removed from the site. For the same reason, one must keep very detailed rec-ords of the excavation and everything found in it. It is not only amazingly easy to forget even the more obvious facts after an interval of several months, but also, what seems insignificant at the time might assume great importance when the material is being analyzed in the laboratory. Archaeology is a "destructive" science in that once a site is excavated it can never be replaced, and unless proper care and accuracy are maintained a great deal of valuable information can be irretrievably lost. Theoretically, when an archaeologist finishes his fieldwork, he or anyone else should be able to "put everything back" in its original position on the basis of his records. To help insure this, the site is staked out with markers prior to excavation, and these provide controls for the excavation to follow.

Most excavations are laid out in a grid system of individually numbered squares. Each square is dug separately and all specimens are catalogued according to specific squares and depths. Usually the earth is stripped off with hand tools in layers that either are of equal thickness or follow natural soil strata within the deposit. Depth measurement is rigidly controlled from a number of permanent markers placed over and around the excavation. If a grid system is too cumbersome, as in a very large site with scattered building foundations, a triangulation method is employed, and all artifacts and features (such as hearths, burials, or architectural remains) are located on the maps and notes by measurements taken from two or more permanent control points. As the material is taken out, it is catalogued in such a way as to describe its exact position in the site, and numerous drawings and photographs are made to supplement the record. From the catalogue, illustrations, and field notes, one should be able to unfold the archaeological data from the excavation and to determine the precise spatial relationships of all materials found.

The next step is to describe and classify all the data recovered. This is by far the most time-consuming part of the archaeologist's work. All artifacts are divided into categories, or types, on the basis of size, shape, decoration, function, raw material, and so forth. The typological classification permits the determination of cultural relationships, provides information on chronological placement, and illustrates the activities of the site's prehistoric inhabitants. Floral and faunal debris as well as geological evidence is analyzed to help date the site and reconstruct the prehistoric environment. Animal bones and vegetation or pollen also are used to ascertain subsistence patterns, that is, to tell whether the people depended mostly on seafoods or game, lived mainly on plant foods, or practiced cultivation and animal husbandry. If burials occurred, their sites might shed some light on rituals and beliefs, as might associated architecture, sculpture, or rock art.

A broader but no less important aspect of archaeology is that of placing the already-classified materials from each different excavation into one or more cultures and then comparing the aggregate results to get a good perspective of cultures and culture change through time and space. One might say that the ultimate goal of archaeology is to build a global framework in which all evidence relating to prehistoric man can be placed. In this sense, archaeology can be defined not only as history, but also as the ethnography and ethnology of extinct cultures.

At the present time, a variety of classification schemes are employed for arranging cultural sequences in different areas. Some attempts have been made to work out a universal taxonomic system, but thus far no great amount of agreement has been achieved among archaeologists. In much of the Old World, the classic descriptive terminology is based on the primary materials used for tool manufacture, hence the names "Stone Age," "Bronze Age," and "Iron Age." The so-called Stone Age is subdivided into Lower, Middle, and Upper Paleolithic (Stone Age cultures of the Pleistocene geological period), Mesolithic (post-Pleistocene Stone Age before agriculture had appeared), and Neolithic (when agriculture was practiced but no metal was used).

Not all areas went through this sequence within the same time periods; some areas did not even go through the same sequence. Africa, for example, had no Bronze Age outside Egypt, and most of the continent had no Neolithic period, properly speaking. The Bronze Age began between 4000-3000 B. C. in the Near East, but did not occur until about 1800 B. C. or later in temperate Europe. Moreover, the sharing of the same age-name does not mean that the areas also share the same stage of cultural advancement. The "Bronze Age" in the Near East connotes not only metal use but also the beginnings of urban civilization, commerce, and literacy. In most of Europe, it implies little more than the use of copper and bronze for tools and weapons. In sub-Saharan Africa, somewhat different terms designate subdivisions of the Stone Age. "Earlier Stone Age" is the equivalent of Europe's Lower and Middle Paleolithic; "Middle Stone Age" describes cultures of the same time period as the Upper Paleolithic; and "Later Stone Age" is used for the cultures of the Mesolithic. In America, different terminology prevails in the eastern United States, the Southwest, and Latin America. This is partly out of tradition and partly because the cultures in these different areas are not very comparable.

Clearly, some improvements are needed, and broader classifications probably should be based on subsistence and settlement types rather than on tool types and raw materials. Before this can be done, however, we require much more intensive work in many regions and a better understanding of prehistoric cultural processes as a whole. Even then, it seems unlikely that we can ever hope for more than a very generally descriptive system of nomenclature inasmuch as cultural change was seldom uniform. Many alternatives were open to prehistoric man just as to modern man. In short, it appears that students of archaeology will have to put up with terminological confusion for some time to come.

INTRODUCTION

Much yet remains to be learned of human evolution—the step-by-step process through which we have progressed from some apelike ancestor to our present status. The evidence for evolution comes from the fossil bones of ancient man in Africa, Asia, and Europe. Preservation of these remains, as well as their discovery by modern scientists, has been largely a matter of chance, and therefore some specific problems are still unsolved. Nevertheless, the general course of human physical development can be fairly well documented with the fossils we have at hand, and periodically new specimens are recovered to further extend our knowledge.

Man's ancestors can be traced back into the earlier part of Pleistocene, the Ice Age of the Northern Hemisphere and its less frigid equivalents in tropical and subtropical areas. Four major groups, if not stages, of early men and near-men have been recognized. The Australopithecines, or man-apes, of early Pleistocene Africa have been found in several localities in the Transvaal region of South Africa and, more recently, in geological deposits of northern Tanganyika in East Africa. These creatures must have lived nearly a million years ago; so primitive are they that we are not quite certain whether to term them *human* or not. The second group, the Pithecanthropines, are of Middle Pleistocene date (approximately 500,000 years old) and are true humans of the genus *Homo*. They are known primarily from Javanese and Chinese fossils (Java man and Peking man), although representatives of the same type have been found in both East and North Africa. Predominantly early Upper Pleistocene in date (perhaps 50,000-150,000 years old) is the Neanderthaloid phase, which has been defined mostly on the basis of fossils from

11

Europe and the Near East. Similar forms, however, have been discovered in Africa and the Far East. Finally, near the close of the Ice Age our own species, *Homo sapiens* appears. There are those who contend that he made his debut much earlier than this, possibly even before Neanderthal man, but the evidence for it is not completely convincing.[1]

The question of how man came to differ from lower animals must have crossed the mind of nearly every person at one time or another. Even the anthropologist cannot give a full answer to this query, but archaeological and paleontological research is beginning to throw some light on the processes involved.

Any explanation of human origins must be couched in terms of intimate and reciprocal relationships between biology, culture, and environment. Without the human organism, no such thing as culture exists; without culture, human society is unimaginable; and man as a culture-building animal always has to adapt himself to a physical setting. The following selection considers some of the functional correlations between three of man's outstanding characteristics—erect posture, intelligence, and toolmaking—with these facts in mind. Traditionally, anthropologists have thought that these three traits appeared simultaneously or that bipedal locomotion and a large brain led to the consistent use and manufacture of tools and weapons. It is now suspected, largely on the basis of information on the erect, small-brained man-apes of Africa, that bipedalism, by freeing the hands, led a ground-dwelling primate of this kind almost immediately to habitual use of tools as a matter of survival. This, in turn, promoted far-reaching changes in intelligence, anatomy, and social behavior.

$$\Diamond \qquad \Diamond \qquad \Diamond$$

A series of recent discoveries has linked prehuman primates of half a million years ago with stone tools. For some years investigators had been uncovering tools of the simplest kind from ancient deposits in

Sherwood F. Washburn, "Tools and Human Evolution." *Scientific American* 203(1960):63-75. Copyright © 1960 by Scientific American, Inc. All rights reserved. Reprinted by permission of *Scientific American* and the author.

[1] Dr. L. S. B. Leakey has recently reported the discovery of several fragmentary fossils in Australopithecine-bearing deposits in Tanganyika. These have been named *Homo habilus* and may be more direct forerunners of modern man than the Australopithecines according to their discoverer. Continued work at the site of these finds should clarify the claims that have been made concerning their advanced anatomical appearance at so early a date.

Africa. At first they assumed that these tools constituted evidence of the existence of large-brained, fully bipedal men. Now the tools have been found in association with much more primitive creatures, the not-fully bipedal, small-brained near-men, or man-apes. Prior to these finds the prevailing view held that man evolved nearly to his present structural state and then discovered tools and the new ways of life that they made possible. Now it appears that man-apes—creatures able to run but not yet walk on two legs, and with brains no larger than those of apes now living—had already learned to make and to use tools. It follows that the structure of modern man must be the result of the change in the terms of natural selection that came with the tool-using way of life.

The earliest stone tools are chips or simple pebbles, usually from river gravels. Many of them have not been shaped at all, and they can be identified as tools only because they appear in concentrations, along with a few worked pieces, in caves or other locations where no such stones naturally occur. The huge advantage that a stone tool gives to its user must be tried to be appreciated. Held in the hand, it can be used for pounding, digging or scraping. Flesh and bone can be cut with a flaked chip, and what would be a mild blow with the fist becomes lethal with a rock in the hand. Stone tools can be employed, moreover, to make tools of other materials. Naturally occurring sticks are nearly all rotten, too large, or of inconvenient shape; some tool for fabrication is essential for the efficient use of wood. The utility of a mere pebble seems so limited to the user of modern tools that it is not easy to comprehend the vast difference that separates the tool-user from the ape which relies on hands and teeth alone. Ground-living monkeys dig out roots for food, and if they could use a stone or a stick, they might easily double their food supply. It was the success of the simplest tools that started the whole trend of human evolution and led to the civilizations of today.

From the short-term point of view, human structure makes human behavior possible. From the evolutionary point of view, behavior and structure form an interacting complex, with each change in one affecting the other. Man began when populations of apes, about a million years ago, started the bipedal, tool-using way of life that gave rise to the man-apes of the genus *Australopithecus*. Most of the obvious differences that distinguish man from ape came after the use of tools.

The primary evidence for the new view of human evolution is teeth, bones and tools. But our ancestors were not fossils; they were striving creatures, full of rage, dominance and the will to live. What evolved was the pattern of life of intelligent, exploratory, playful, vigorous primates; the evolving reality was a succession of social systems based upon the motor abilities, emotions and intelligence of their members. Selection produced new systems of child care, maturation and sex, just as it did alterations in the skull and the teeth. Tools, hunting, fire, complex social life, speech, the human way and the brain evolved together to produce ancient man of the genus *Homo* about half a million years ago. Then the brain evolved under the pressures of more complex social life until the species *Homo sapiens* appeared perhaps as recently as 50,000 years ago.

With the advent of *Homo sapiens* the tempo of technical-social evolution quickened. Some of the early types of tool had lasted for hundreds of thousands of years and were essentially the same throughout vast areas of the African and Eurasian land masses. Now the tool forms multiplied and became regionally diversified. Man invented the bow, boats, clothing; conquered the Arctic; invaded the New World; domesticated plants and animals; discovered metals, writing and civilization. Today, in the midst of the latest tool-making revolution, man has achieved the capacity to adapt his environment to his need and impulse, and his numbers have begun to crowd the planet.

This article is concerned with the beginnings of the process by which, as Theodosius Dobzhansky says, biological evolution has transcended itself. From the rapidly accumulating evidence it is now possible to speculate with some confidence on the manner in which the way of life made possible by tools changed the pressures of natural selection and so changed the structure of man.

Tools have been found, along with the bones of their makers, at Sterkfontein, Swartkrans and Kromdraai in South Africa, and at Olduvai in Tanganyika. Many of the tools from Sterkfontein are merely unworked river pebbles, but someone had to carry them from the gravels some miles away and bring them to the deposit in which they are found. Nothing like them occurs naturally in the local limestone caves. Of course the association of the stone tools with man-ape bones in one or two localities does not prove that these animals made the tools. It has been argued that a more advanced form of man, already present, was the toolmaker. This argument has a familiar ring to students of human evolution. Peking man was thought too primitive to be a toolmaker; when the first manlike pelvis was found with man-ape bones, some argued that it must have fallen into the deposit because it was too human to be associated with the skull. In

every case, however, the repeated discovery of the same unantici-
pated association has ultimately settled the controversy.

This is why the discovery by L. S. B. and Mary Leakey in the summer of 1959 is so important. In Olduvai Gorge in Tanganyika they
came upon traces of an old living site, and found stone tools in clear
association with the largest man-ape skull known. With the stone
tools were a hammer stone and waste flakes from the manufacture of
the tools. The deposit also contained the bones of rats, mice, frogs,
and some bones of juvenile pig and antelope, showing that even the
largest and latest of the man-apes could kill only the smallest animals
and must have been largely vegetarian. The Leakeys' discovery
confirms the association of the man-ape with pebble tools, and adds
the evidence of manufacture to that of mere association. Moreover,
the stratigraphic evidence at Olduvai now for the first time securely
dates the man-apes, placing them in the Lower Pleistocene, earlier
than 500,000 years ago and earlier than the first skeletal and cultural
evidence for the existence of the genus *Homo*. Before the discovery
at Olduvai these points had been in doubt.

The man-apes themselves are known from several skulls and a
large number of teeth and jaws, but only fragments of the rest of the
skeleton have been preserved. There were two kinds of man-ape, a
small early one that may have weighed 50 or 60 pounds and a later
and larger one that weighed at least twice as much. The differences
in size and form between the two types are quite comparable to the
differences between the contemporary pygmy chimpanzee and the
common chimpanzee.

Pelvic remains from both forms of man-ape show that these animals were bipedal. From a comparison of the pelvis of ape, man-ape,
and man it can be seen that the upper part of the pelvis is much
wider and shorter in man than in the ape, and that the pelvis of the
man-ape corresponds closely, though not precisely, to that of modern
man. The long upper pelvis of the ape is characteristic of most mammals, and it is the highly specialized, short, wide bone in man that
makes possible the human kind of bipedal locomotion. Although the
man-ape pelvis is apelike in its lower part, it approaches that of man
in just those features that distinguish man from all other animals.
More work must be done before this combination of features is fully
understood. My belief is that bipedal running, made possible by the
changes in the upper pelvis, came before efficient bipedal walking,
made possible by the changes in the lower pelvis. In the man-ape,
therefore, the adaptation to bipedal locomotion is not yet complete.

Here, then is a phase of human evolution characterized by forms that are mostly bipedal, small-brained, plains-living, tool-making hunters of small animals.

The capacity for bipedal walking is primarily an adaptation for covering long distances. Even the arboreal chimpanzee can run faster than a man, and any monkey can easily outdistance him. A man, on the other hand, can walk for many miles, and this is essential for efficient hunting. According to skeletal evidence, fully developed walkers first appeared in the ancient men [Pithecanthropines and Neanderthaloids] who inhabited the Old World from 500,000 years ago to the middle of the last glaciation. These men were competent hunters, as is shown by the bones of the large animals they killed. But they also used fire and made complicated tools according to clearly defined traditions. Along with the change in the structure of the pelvis, the brain had doubled in size since the time of the man-apes.

The fossil record thus substantiates the suggestion, first made by Charles Darwin, that tool use is both the cause and the effect of bipedal locomotion. Some very limited bipedalism left the hands sufficiently free from locomotor functions so that stones or sticks could be carried, played with and used. The advantage that these objects gave to their users led both to more bipedalism and to more efficient tool use. English lacks any neat expression for this sort of situation, forcing us to speak of cause and effect as if they were separated, whereas in natural selection cause and effect are interrelated. Selection is based on successful behavior, and in the man-apes the beginnings of the human way of life depended on both inherited locomotor capacity and on the learned skills of tool-using. The success of the new way of life based on the use of tools changed the selection pressures on many parts of the body, notably the teeth, hands and brain, as well as on the pelvis. But it must be remembered that selection was for the whole way of life.

In all the apes and monkeys the males have large canine teeth. The long upper canine cuts against the first lower premolar, and the lower canine passes in front of the upper canine. This is an efficient fighting mechanism, backed by very large jaw muscles. I have seen male baboons drive off cheetahs and dogs, and according to reliable reports male baboons have even put leopards to flight. The females have small canines, and they hurry away with the young under the very conditions in which the males turn to fight. All the evidence from living monkeys and apes suggests that the male's large canines are of the greatest importance to the survival of the group, and that they are particularly important in ground-living forms that may not be able to climb to safety in the trees. The small, early man-apes lived in open plains country, and yet none of them had large canine teeth. It would appear that the protection of the group must have shifted from teeth to tools early in the evolution of the man-apes, and long before the appearance of the forms that have been found in association with stone tools. The tools of Sterkfontein and Olduvai represent not the beginnings of tool use, but a choice of material and knowledge in manufacture which, as is shown by the small canines of the man-apes that deposited them there, derived from a long history of tool use.

Reduction in the canine teeth is not a simple matter, but involves changes in the muscles, face, jaws and other parts of the skull. Selection builds powerful neck muscles in animals that fight with their canines, and adapts the skull to the action of these muscles. Fighting is not a matter of teeth alone, but also of seizing, shaking, and hurling an enemy's body with the jaws, head, and neck. Reduction in the canines is therefore accompanied by a shortening in the jaws, reduction in the ridges of bone over the eyes, and a decrease in the shelf of bone in the neck area. The reason that the skulls of the females and young of the apes look more like man-apes than those of adult males is that, along with small canines, they have smaller muscles and all the numerous structural features that go along with them. The skull of the man-ape is that of an ape that has lost the structure for effective fighting with its teeth. Moreover, the man-ape has transferred to its hands the functions of seizing and pulling, and this has been attended by reduction of its incisors. Small canines and incisors are biological symbols of a changed way of life; their primitive functions are replaced by hand and tool.

The history of the grinding teeth—the molars—is different from that of the seizing and fighting teeth. Large size in any anatomical structure must be maintained by positive selection; the selection pressure changed first on the canine teeth and, much later, on the molars. In the man-apes the molars were very large, larger than in either ape or man. They were heavily worn, possibly because food dug from the ground with the aid of tools was very abrasive. With the men of the Middle Pleistocene, molars of human size appear along with complicated tools, hunting, and fire.

The disappearance of brow ridges and the refinement of the human face may involve still another factor. One of the essential conditions for the organization of men in cooperative societies was the suppression of rage and of the uncontrolled drive to first place in the hierarchy of dominance. Recently it has been shown that domestic animals, chosen over the generations for willingness to adjust and for lack of rage, have relatively small adrenal glands, as Curt P. Richter of John Hopkins University has shown. But the breeders who selected for this hormonal, physiological, temperamental type also picked, without realizing it, animals with small brow ridges and small faces. The skull structure of the wild rat bears the same relation to that of the tame rat as does the skull of Neanderthal man to that of *Homo sapiens*. The same is true for the cat, dog, pig, horse, and cow; in each case the wild form has the larger face and muscular ridges. In the later stages of human evolution, it appears, the self-domestication of man has been exerting the same effects upon temperament, glands, and skull that are seen in the domestic animals.

Of course from man-ape to man the brain-containing part of the skull has also increased greatly in size. This change is directly due to the increase in the size of the brain: as the brain grows, so grow the bones that cover it. Since there is this close correlation between brain size and bony brain-case, the brain size of the fossils can be estimated. On the scale of brain size the man-apes are scarcely distinguishable from the living apes, although their brains may have been larger with respect to body size. The brain seems to have evolved rapidly, doubling in size between man-ape and man. It then appears to have increased much more slowly; there is no substantial change in gross size during the last 100,000 years. One must remember, however, that size alone is a very crude indicator, and that brains of equal size may vary greatly in function. My belief is that although the brain of *Homo sapiens* is no larger than that of Neanderthal man, the indirect evidence strongly suggests that the first *Homo sapiens* was a much more intelligent creature.

The great increase in brain size is important because many functions of the brain seem to depend on the number of cells, and the number increases with volume. But certain parts of the brain have increased in size much more than others. As functional maps of the cortex of the brain show, the human sensory-motor cortex is not just an enlargement of that of an ape. The areas for the hand, especially the thumb, in man are tremendously enlarged, and this is an integral part of the structural base that makes the skillful use of the hand possible. The selection pressures that favored a large thumb also favored a large cortical area to receive sensations from the thumb and to control its motor activity. Evolution favored the development of a sensitive, powerful, skillful thumb, and in all these ways—as well as in structure—a human thumb differs from that of an ape.

The same is true for other cortical areas. Much of the cortex in a monkey is still engaged in the motor and sensory functions. In man it is the areas adjacent to the primary centers that are most expanded. These areas are concerned with skills, memory, foresight and language; that is, with the mental faculties that make human social life possible. This is easiest to illustrate in the field of language. Many apes and monkeys can make a wide variety of sounds. These sounds do not, however, develop into language. Some workers have devoted great efforts, with minimum results, to trying to teach chimpanzees to talk. The reason is that there is little in the brain to teach. A human child learns to speak with the greatest ease, but the storage of thousands of words takes a great deal of cortex. Even the simplest language must have given great advantage to those first men who had it. One is tempted to think that language may have appeared together with the fine tools, fire, and complex hunting of the large-brained men of the Middle Pleistocene, but there is no direct proof of this.

The main point is that the kind of animal that can learn to adjust to complex, human, technical society is a very different creature from a tree-living ape, and the differences between the two are rooted in the evolutionary process. The reason that the human brain makes the human way of life possible is that it is the result of that way of life. Great masses of the tissue in the human brain are devoted to memory, planning, language, and skills, because these are the abilities favored by the human way of life.

The emergence of man's large brain occasioned a profound change in the plan of human reproduction. The human mother-child relationship is unique among the primates as is the use of tools. In all the apes and monkeys the baby clings to the mother; to be able to do so, the baby must be born with its central nervous system in an advanced state of development. But the brain of the fetus must be small enough so that birth may take place. In man adaptation to bipedal locomotion decreased the size of the bony birth-canal at the same time that the exigencies of tool use selected for larger brains. This obstretrical dilemma was solved by delivery of the fetus at a much earlier stage of development. But this was possible only because the mother, already bipedal and with hands free of locomotor necessities, could hold the helpless, immature infant. The small-brained man-ape probably developed in the uterus as much as the ape does; the human type of mother-child relation must have evolved by the time of the large-brained, fully bipedal humans of the Middle Pleistocene. Bipedalism, tool use, and selection for large brains thus slowed human development and invoked far greater maternal responsibility. The slow-moving mother, carrying the baby, could not hunt, and the combination of the woman's obligation to care for slow-developing babies and the man's occupation of hunting imposed a fundamental pattern on the social organization of the human species.

All these family functions are ultimately related to tools, hunting, and the enlargement of the brain. Complex and technical society evolved from the sporadic tool-using of an ape, through the simple pebble tools of the man-ape and the complex toolmaking traditions of ancient men to the hugely complicated culture of modern man. Each behavioral stage was both cause and effect of biological change in bones and brain. These concomitant changes can be seen in the scanty fossil record and can be inferred from the study of the living forms.

Surely as more fossils are found these ideas will be tested. New techniques of investigation, from planned experiments in the behavior of lower primates to more refined methods of dating, will extract wholly new information from the past. It is my belief that, as these events come to pass, tool use will be found to have been a major factor, beginning with the initial differentiation of man and ape. In ourselves we see a structure, physiology and behavior that is the result of the fact that some populations of apes started to use tools a million years ago. The pebble tools constituted man's principal technical adaptation for a period of least 50 times as long as recorded history. As we contemplate man's present eminence, it is well to remember that, from the point of view of evolution, the events of the last 50,000 years occupy but a moment in time. Ancient man endured at least 10 times as long and the man-apes for an even longer time.

INTRODUCTION

We have just been shown something of the threshold over which our remote ancestors passed in their transition from nonhuman to human beings about one million years ago, with an attempt to explain just how and why this turning point was reached. Other scientists have outlined for us the various stages of further development in human physical characteristics and cultural achievements over hundreds of thousands of years before modern-looking, if still primitive, men entered the scene about 40,000 to 50,000 years ago, or 48,000-38,000 B. C. This whole process of change, leading from small roving bands of food-scavenging man-apes to well-organized groups of proficient big-game hunters, accounts for at least 90 per cent of our existence and is known to archaeologists as the Lower Paleolithic.

During most of this period, cultural development was extremely slow, and conservatism the order of the day. In some instances, almost identical stone tools were made and used for thousands upon thousands of years without noticeable change. Nevertheless, man did learn to adapt himself to his surroundings, and probably had begun to take notice of the larger universe around him. Though we know of Paleolithic man largely through stone implements which have survived because of their relative indestructibility, he also must have made use of wood, bone, antler, and other more perishable raw materials. There is evidence, for example, that sharpened staves of wood were employed as spears, and it is possible that before the end of this era, hunting was made more effective by the construction of game pits, traps, or deadfalls. The kinds of stone implements from this period are few and simple; most of them probably served as all-purpose tools for cutting, scraping, gouging, and digging. The earliest of these—the so-called pebble tools—are no more than water-worn stones with a few flakes struck off one end to provide a sharp point and a rough edge for chopping or skinning. Pebble tools have been found only in Africa, where they eventually evolved into more easily recognizable implements such as the hand axe, or biface, which is a more or less pear-shaped artifact with a pointed tip, carefully flaked over both surfaces. In an early stage of development, the hand-axe tradition spread to Europe and southwest Asia and, as in Africa, persisted for approximately 350,000 years.

One of the most significant discoveries of Lower Paleolithic man was the use and control of fire. The consequences of this were of even greater magnitude than those envisioned in Charles Lamb's essay on roast pig, for cooking food was but a minor application of this new tool. More importantly, it afforded warmth and protection. With fire (and perhaps clothing, although we have no proof of it), man as a basically tropical primate was able to invade new and colder latitudes in Europe and Asia. It is only at this point that we can begin to speak of "cave dwellers," since the use of fire appears to have been a prerequisite to establishing one's home in these natural shelters. Caves are not only cold and damp, but in those times could house saber-toothed cats or cave bears as well as humans. Fire would have mitigated such difficulties considerably.

The first evidence we have for the use of fire is in northern China, where hearths in a cave occupied by Pithecanthropines date to the middle of the Pleistocene, perhaps 200,000 to 300,000 years ago. In Africa and Europe, the control of fire and cave dwelling are not indicated until toward the end of the Lower Paleolithic (40,000 to 50,000 years ago).

Neanderthal man in Europe, along with some of his contemporaries elsewhere, not only used fire but also made some modest improvements in stone-tool technology. Among the artifacts found in his habitation sites are spearheads that possibly represent the first stone implements hafted on handles or shafts. It is also among Neanderthalers that we can identify the earliest glimmerings of supernatural beliefs. These ancient Europeans carefully interred their dead, which implies some concern with life after death and perhaps even a fear of spirits. It has been argued that hunting magic is discernible in some sort of cave-bear cult suggested by piles of skulls found in central European caves; however, not everyone agrees with this interpretation.

The way of life followed by men of the Lower Paleolithic must have been simple and austere. The size and distribution of their campsites indicate that populations were small and scattered—each local group being no larger than a single family or small band of related families. That no single encampment caused the formation of a thick deposit of debris shows that these people were migratory, never staying for long at one place. Their rather generalized hunting-and-gathering mode of subsistence would have required that each little band have a very substantial territory in order that it might eke out a living with its limited technology. The more difficult habitats, such as rain forest or tundra, were still less densely inhabited or avoided altogether. It seems likely that the total population of even such relatively congenial environments as Spain or East Africa would have numbered in the hundreds rather than in the thousands. Yet the stage was set for humanity to come, for the mainstream of human evolution had been traversed and man had established his dominance over all other forms of animal life.

During a temporary recession of the northern ice sheets in the final glacial period of the Pleistocene, the Neanderthal was replaced by *Homo sapiens,* who possessed a greatly superior technology (whether this superiority had any biological foundation is debatable). To this fact we may possibly credit the rapid spread of anatomically modern man and his eradication or absorption of his forerunners. In this final Pelistocene period, the Upper Paleolithic food-collectors adapted themselves to what were then steppes and tundras through the specialized and often selective hunting of large herbivores such as mammoth, bison, wild horse, or reindeer. Game drives and other types of highly organized communal hunting as well as new weapons, such as the bow and arrow and the harpoon, made selective hunting an efficient means of making a living, which in turn probably promoted population growth and increased economic stability. Before the close of the Ice Age, new areas were opened to human occupation. Australia appears to have been first inhabited during this time, and Soviet archaeologists tell us that only then are there traces of man in Siberia. Once in Siberia, Upper Paleolithic hunters were able to cross over into America via the Bering Strait to open up a whole new hemisphere.

At the beginning of the modern geological era, about ten thousand years ago, or 8,000 B. C., Upper Paleolithic cultures in temperate Europe and Asia gave way to Mesolithic hunters and food-gatherers who were making an adjustment to warmer postglacial conditions. Steppe and tundra were yielding to forestation; the large mammals of the Pleistocene were replaced by fleeter-footed modern animals that could not afford man as lucrative a hunting life as he enjoyed previously. As a result, fishing, shellfish-collecting, and gathering of wild vegetable products were pursued more strenuously in order to obtain enough food. The magnificent graphic and plastic art traditions of the Upper Paleolithic, discussed in some detail below, died out completely, probably because they were tied so closely to the now-extinct game animals upon which life had previously depended. About the only notable innovations were the development of heavy woodworking tools and the manufacture of microlithic flints, very small blades or geometric forms that were mounted with natural adhesives in wood or bone shafts to serve as barbs or multiple cutting edges. The composite tool had arrived.

By the time these new food-collecting economies were taking shape in Europe, comparable groups in Southwest Asia were already beginning to experiment with the plant and animal domestication that would eventually open entirely different vistas to man.

It is not difficult to reconstruct the technology and economy of Paleolithic societies, but more imagination is required to visualize what life meant to these people. Virtually nothing can be said concerning the very earliest men in this respect, simply because the available evidence is solely of a technological order. However, by the time of the Neanderthalers we begin to find some hints of a belief system, and the cave art and sculpture of the Upper Paleolithic provides us with our first really good glimpse of nonmaterial culture in prehistory.

◇　　◇　　◇

Like most other learned or scientific subjects, archaeology has its traditional lore centering upon famous events and personalities in its history. One of the best loved of all these tales is the one about Don Marcelino de Sautuola and his young daughter and their discovery of the Altamira cave paintings—the first important group of Paleolithic paintings to be made known. Everyone has heard how, while her father was busy excavating the cave floor, the girl, with the ignorant and therefore quick eyes of childhood, saw the great bison paintings on the roof and ran to her father crying, Toros! Toros! Not so much is said about the unhappy sequence to this happy discovery. Don Marcelino was savagely attacked by the learned world, led by the eminent French archaeologist Cartailhac,

Jacquetta Hawkes, "Paleolithic Art." From *History Today*, VIII (1958), 10-16, 98-102. Reprinted by permission of the author.

and was even accused of having the paintings faked by a dumb artist whom he had befriended. The pride of a Spanish nobleman prevented him from fighting back as Boucher de Perthes and many other pioneers had to do, and he died with the authenticity of this wonderful painted cave still in doubt.

This is a shocking story—one sometimes feels that experts have a genius for swallowing fakes and refusing the authentic; yet it is easy to understand the stubborn resistance put up by Cartailhac and his learned colleagues. The existence of Paleolithic painting was so very unlikely. Indeed, in the present writer's eyes, this flowering of the visual arts among the hunting peoples of Ice-Age Europe was the most improbable event in all human history.

Fully to appreciate this improbability, we have to consider the background, both geographical and historical. The art was created by a number of Upper Paleolithic (Late Old Stone Age) peoples with distinct but broadly related cultural traditions. How long it flourished is still unknown; but it must have been for at least twenty thousand years, roughly from 30,000-10,000 B.C. The whole of these twenty millennia coincided with the last of the four great glacial phases of Pleistocene times, when glaciers spread far down from the summits of the Alps and Pyrenees and huge ice sheets covered most of northern Europe. There were fluctuations in the climate certainly, periods when it warmed up enough greatly to affect the wild life, as is clearly reflected in the varying species of animals depicted by the artists. Nevertheless, we have to picture these big game hunters as living in their caves during winters sometimes severe, sometimes sub-arctic, with land and water frozen like iron, the very elephants (mammoth) and rhinoceros growing hairy coats against the frosts and ice-sharp winds. Even allowing for the fact that game was plentiful, and that by the end of the period the women were stitching good leather clothing, these are not conditions in which modern artists would care to work, or in which one would expect artistic genius to make its first appearance on earth.

If his surroundings were discouraging, man's own past did not look promising. For something like half a million years his cultural development had been so slow that a hundred generations might live and die without making any perceptible progress. There had, it is true, been some acceleration during the warmer interval before the last advance of the ice. But, at the end of this interval, a time when the somewhat brutal-looking and culturally uninventive Neanderthal breed was dominant in Europe, there were few signs of the great things soon to come.

There may, of course, have been faint intimations of man's future as an artist. From near the beginning of his life as a tool-maker, he may have collected objects pleasing to his eye—such as the quartz crystals found in the cave dwelling of Peking man. He may have decked himself with flowers and colored feathers—and, more to the point, have painted designs on his own body. Again, the finest early Paleolithic tools have a perfection of form and workmanship suggestive of an innate aesthetic sense in their makers. Then we have to remember that there may have been an approach to artistic creation through activities that can leave no trace behind them; it is quite probable that well before Upper Paleolithic time small tribal groups had begun to dance and to chant.

Even allowing for all such faint premonitions of artistic powers, their sudden upsurge thirty thousand years ago remains a staggering improbability. Yet it happened. As the last glaciation gripped Europe, the Neanderthal breed died out and was replaced by races of modern type. Skill and adaptiveness in developing material culture made them highly successful hunters, and before long—we do not know just how long—they began their career as artists. Their best work can be favorably compared with anything achieved since; it will always remain a happy reminder of the truth that, although art becomes more subtle and complex in content, as pure imaginative expression it does not "progress."

Nearly all the finest Paleolithic cave art comes from three regions in western Europe. One is in south-west France with a center in Dordogne; one on the French slopes of the Pyrenees in and adjoining the departments of Ariège and Haute Garonne; and the third in the Cantabrian mountains of northern Spain. It is with this great Franco-Cantabrian school that we shall be mainly concerned; but something must also be said, even if only to point a contrast, of a quite distinct school of painting found in open rock-shelters along the eastern Spanish coast. Although the earliest works may overlap in age with the more famous group, these East Spanish paintings are mostly later, dating from the subsequent Mesolithic age.

Any true picture of the Franco-Cantabrian school must include, beside the cave murals, the many *objets d'art* found among the domestic rubbish on the cave floors. Some of these are in the form of carved bone, antler and ivory implements, particularly spear-throwers, while others are carvings and engravings of no practical use. Small though many of them are, these pieces number among them some of the most exquisite masterpieces of Paleolithic art.

The setting in which it is found is important for any understanding of this art. When the hunters and their families took up their winter quarters in a cave, they did not live in the depths, but near the entrance, where light could enter and smoke escape, and where they were safe from the cave lions and bears that lurked in the long galleries and lofty caverns running far into the limestone rock. Here by the domestic hearth they kept their carved spear-throwers and the other small treasures already described; but it was not here that the artists executed their murals. There are, it is true, a few sites such as Cap Blanc, l'Angles-sur-l'Anglin and Pair non Pair where the hunters lived beside sculptures and paintings. But this is exceptional. A very large proportion of cave art occurs in uninhabited caverns, and much of it in those inner fastnesses that can have been regularly visited only by wild beasts.

Many paintings and engravings are in situations that must have been extraordinarily difficult to reach, involving the negotiation of dangerous chasms, waterfalls and narrow fissures. When it is remembered the artists had first to explore these eerie underground warrens, and then to set to work by the light of tiny fat or blubber lamps, it is evident that there was some significance in their choice of sites. They deliberately sought cave walls far removed from the familiar outdoor world and the domestic life of the cave entry.

Not the least remarkable element in the total achievement of the artists was their rapid development of a wide range of artistic techniques. They invented drawing, engraving, stencilling, painting, modelling in relief and in the round, and sculpture in relief and in the round—almost every process known to us today. This fact is in itself of general interest; for it shows how quickly the human brain will invent new technical skills if it is responding to a well-defined challenge. Paleolithic art was almost certainly the work of specialists —that is to say, of gifted individuals who were freed from some part of their social responsibility as hunters. They may perhaps have formed an artists' clan, such as existed among the African Bushmen. Men like these must have become fully conscious of technical problems of their art and made up their minds to solve them. So, at the very beginning of artistic creation, we find this astonishing inventiveness.

It is worth while to go a little more fully into this aspect of the subject, partly to convey some idea of these pioneers inventing their implements, searching their surroundings for materials, partly to introduce a few of the finest examples of each form and so give an impression of the range of subjects that were treated.

For engraving and carving, a variety of small flint tools was perfected. The most specialized were chisels and gouges with sharp, strong cutting edges; awls and ordinary flint knives and scrapers may also have been used by the sculptors. As for the painters, there are signs that they sometimes worked with brushes which they may have made, like certain modern primitive peoples, by chewing the ends of fibrous sticks. Outlines might also be drawn with the finger tip dipped in pigment, or with sharpened quills and sticks; for big color washes pads of fur or moss were used; or, occasionally, these pads were very effectively employed for dabbing on color in a kind of stump work technique. A few paintings, such as the lovely "Chinese horses" at Lascaux, show such smoothly graduated shading that it seems they may have been executed with some simple form of spray. Perhaps by blowing powdered paint through a tube on to a prepared fatty surface, or by squirting liquid color through the lips. It is almost certain this latter, rather distasteful, method accounts for the negative hand-impressions that are among the oldest form of cave painting; the open hand would have been applied to the cave wall and the color squirted round it to make an image that is in fact a form of stencil.

As for the pigments used, they were nearly all natural minerals. The most popular were oxides of iron, ranging in color from chocolate to light red, orange and yellow. Oxides of manganese gave a brown and a blue-black, while burnt bone or soot might be used for carbon blacks. These pigments were ground to a fine powder, sometimes with specially made pestles and mortars; and the powders were kept in such small containers as stoppered boneshafts, shells and hollow stones. Before application they seem sometimes to have been mixed with a water base, sometimes with fat. A charming bone palette from the Grotte de Rey in the Dordogne, carved in the shape of a fish, may well have served for color-mixing. Rarely the artist may have prepared sticks of mineral colors and used them like crayons. It looks as though a crayon of this kind was used to outline the unfinished rhinoceros in the pit at Lascaux.

Engraving should, perhaps, rank as the simplest of all the techniques, although the use of the specially designed flint gravers lifted it far above mere scratching. Thousands of engravings are found in the French caves, sometimes covering the walls like lace. Combarelles is a famous example in the southwestern group, its walls displaying a great variety of animals—mammoth, bear, ibex, lion and horse—and a few rough sketches of masked men. Some of this is a very late work, and reminds us that simple engravings persisted throughout the whole period. Another well-known cave is Les Trois Frères in the French Pyreneean group, where the pale limestone walls are covered with little engravings of exquisite fineness, some complete animals, but many of them brilliant studies of a single limb, or head, all flung together in a manner highly suggestive of the crowded sketch-book of some Old Master. In Cantabria a distinctive school of engraving developed, in which very fine shading was used to give a sense of roundness. Engraving was often combined with painting, usually to draw the outline, but sometimes to suggest the texture of fur. One of the strangest and best known of all Paleolithic works, the antlered, dancing "Sorcerer" from Les Trois Frères, combines the two techniques; and so do many of the animal studies at Lascaux, Font de Gaume and Altamira.

Engraving was also much practiced on pieces of bone and antler, where it might become deep and bold enough to approach bas-relief. But, with carving in relief, we must return to work on a more monumental scale. Perhaps the two most striking caves where sculptures have been cut directly from the living rock are those of Cap Blanc near Les Eyzies with its magnificent life-size frieze of horses, and l'Angles-sur-l'Anglin (a northern outlier in the Vienne), where three large female figures, lacking heads or feet and with the sexual characters emphasized, are carved side by side with fine renderings of bison, ibex and horse.

At le Roc, in the Dordogne, ibex, bison and reindeer were carved on detached rock slabs that were ranged round a cutting in the hillside, perhaps to make some kind of sanctuary; while at Laussel, one of the most important of all the sculptured sites, the carvings were also on detached slabs; but these had been deliberately laid face downward on the cave floor. The subjects were human beings, the two best preserved being the standing figure of a hunter, and a seated woman with fat hips and belly and pendulous breasts, holding a horn, probably a bison horn, in her right hand. At least in the largest of these works, the Cap Blanc horses, although the surface was finished with gravers and other delicate tools, the rough blocking out from the rock must surely have been done with relatively heavy mauls.

The only surviving piece of relief modelling good enough to be compared with these carvings is the bull and cow bison from the Tuc d'Audubert, a cave immediately adjoining the Trois Frères in the Pyrenees. Here a mass of damp clay had been built up on a slab of rock into the form of the two animals, each about two feet in length. The contours of the muscles are vigorously modelled, the ears and horns pinched up between finger and thumb, and such details as the eyes and mane added with a pointed tool.

The Paleolithic artists were also masters of sculpture in the round; but so far as we know practised it only on a small scale. Two *chef d'oeuvres* are the little horse from near Lourdes and the really marvellous horse's head of reindeer antler from the Mas d'Azil— both caves in the Pyrenees. There are also a number of spear-throwers, in which the body of an animal or bird has been most cunningly adapted to the shape of the hooked butt.

With sculpture in the round, we have to introduce a category of works that stands some way apart from the rest of the Franco-Cantabrian school of art. These are the small female statuettes usually known as "Venuses." They relate to the main tradition, through the female figures of Laussel and l'Angles-sur-l'Anglin, whose voluptuous proportions they share; but they are much more widespread. A famous example carved in hard limestone comes from Willendorf in Austria; another, modelled in a mixture of clay and powdered mammoth bone, from a camp of mammoth hunters at Vestonice in Czechoslovakia. Though in a miserably attenuated form unworthy of the name of Venus, carved bone examples have even been found as far east as the Siberian site of Mal'ta. The best of the small figures from Europe are of high merit—the queen among them being the Venus of Lespugues, a most lovely piece of near-abstract art—but others are hardly more than cult objects or fetishes. Their special significance will be discussed presently.

When we come to painting, there is little need to specify examples. For most people the great painted murals of game animals *are* Paleolithic art; and almost everyone is familiar with the finest of them. Can any historical development of style be established among all these paintings? Obviously enough, if they are spread over anything like the twenty thousand years attributed to them, there must have been coherent development. Yet it is extremly difficult to establish except in the very broadest outline. Bold attempts have been made to prove the existence of two distinct stylistic cycles; an earlier one attributed to the Aurignacian form of Upper Paleolithic culture and a later attributed to the Magdalenian form. It is extremely doubtful whether this elaborate scheme can be justified by the facts. The truth is that, while almost every small *objet d'art* can be dated by the occupation horizon in which it lies, very few murals have any reliable associations. Rubbish on the cave floor need not be of the same age as works of art on the walls. For dating purposes, we have to make do with the relatively few instances in which paintings are partly covered by occupation litter or have fallen down into it, or where access to a painted cave has been blocked by later deposits. Carbon 14 dating of charcoal from Lascaux gave the very suitable date of about 13,500 B.C.; but this, and other results that may come from this method, cannot be accepted as dating the murals with any certainty.

A more straightforward scheme of stylistic development must be preferred. First (and undoubtedly earliest) is a phase with simple outline sketches, the animals usually shown in exact profile with only two legs indicated; they also tend to be lacking in movement, and the eye is often omitted. That at this stage the artists were still beginners, groping towards the solution of elementary problems, is demonstrated most clearly of all in the lack of perspective in the rendering of horns and antlers; they are shown full face, even though the body of the beast is in profile. In the next phase considerably greater mastery has been achieved. The animal subjects are now depicted with all four legs, and their horns or antlers in true perspective; while the painters are already displaying skill in breaking the outlines and varying the breadth of stroke to suggest roundness and solidity. It is probably right to include in this second group paintings in which the whole body is filled in with more or less flat color washes. There follows a stage (corresponding roughly with the earlier Magdalenian culture) in which flat washes were certainly used, often in association with engraving, and the "stump work" style was perfected. Partial or even bi-color washes might be employed to suggest modelling. This leads on to the fourth and last phase, of later Magdalenian times, when the high hunting way of life flourished exceedingly before being quenched by the climatic changes of post-glacial times. This was a period when the artist had attained mastery of polychrome painting, using the range of yellows, reds, browns and black to secure a fully rounded, three dimensional effect. The bodies of the animals were beautifully modulated, with every bone and swelling muscle, every fold and hollow given its full value. Often, too, the painter might add touches of glowing color that had no representational purpose, yet gave life and intensity to his work. This great style reached its climax in the finest of the polychrome bison at Altamira.

The limitations of Paleolithic art are most apparent in its subject matter. Enough examples have already been quoted to emphasize the familiar fact that the Franco-Cantabrian school was predominantly concerned to make portraits of single animals in a style of heightened realism. Scenes or pictorial compositions were very rare; human beings were seldom portrayed, in *painting* almost never. In both these things Franco-Cantabrian art contrasts with the East Spanish paintings where men and women were often depicted and scenes of hunting and ceremonial were favorite subjects.

These generalizations must always remain broadly true; yet it so happens that recent discoveries have tended slightly to modify them. In the depths of the pit at Lascaux (discovered in 1940 but hardly published until after the war) was found what has a good claim to be the first narrative picture in the world. Many people are by now familiar with the scene where a man (schematically drawn) is apparently lying dead, while before him a bison stands in a curiously rigid attitude as though about to fall, its ripped intestines hanging down and a broken spear at its side. Even without attempting to bring the neighboring rhinoceros into the scene, there seems no doubt that this unique picture illustrated some particular event—whether from real life or a campfire epic. It told a story; and this was something altogether new.

Equally revolutionary were the discoveries made at l'Angles-sur-l'Anglin after 1948. First, the three female figures helped to connect the Venus statuettes more closely with the ordinary animal sculpture —but Laussel had already gone some way towards achieving this. Far more unexpected was the head and shoulders portrait of a man executed in paint, engraving and low relief. It is the only more or less realistic portrayal of a human being in all Franco-Cantabrian art. The interest of the finds in this site has helped to call attention to engravings in La Grotte de la Marche about twenty miles away, which include poor, but fairly lively, sketches of women, some of them pregnant, and of men with their sexual organs emphasized and even embellished.

The question of human representation in this art is of great interest. The contrast between the match-stick man at Lascaux and the noble realism of the dying bison is representative. With the exception of the l'Angles-sur-l'Anglin portrait, almost all representations of men are either schematic or childishly crude. The Trois Frères "Sorcerer" might be taken as another exception; for it is full of life and feeling—but it will be argued that it represents a spirit-being rather than a man. It remains true, then, that the artists almost never tried to express the essential character of the human male body in the way that they would express the physical essence of bison and reindeer, ibex or mammoth.

This refusal may perhaps be partly explained by the fear that to draw his image might give his enemies power over the man himself. But surely the main reason must be that the male artist had no passionate emotional interest in his fellows? He was content to make signs for them, instead of an emotionally charged image. The drawings of men come near to pictographic writing.

Turning to the sculptured portrayals of the female form, we are in an altogether different realm of emotional expression. We have already seen how, both in the figurines and the larger carvings, the body was shown fat and often pregnant, while the sexual features were emphasized and the face was usually ignored. At l'Angles the Venuses had no heads at all. Here again, then, the artist did not wish to express the female body with the heightened realism he gave to the animal. But there was no lack of emotion: the finest of the Venuses are highly charged with it. He desired only to show the female erotically and as the source of all abundance—in her he portrayed not woman but fertility. He had, in short, created the great symbol of the Mother Goddess that was to have so long a history among mankind.

These speculations lead us on to the fascinating problem of the meaning and purpose of the art we have been studying. It is a fascinating subject; yet perhaps as a problem it has been exaggerated. There is a long-standing dispute between those who have wished to see this art as undertaken for its own sake—for self-expression and the creation of beauty—and those sturdy rationalists who see it as a purely practical activity undertaken to secure good hunting. This conflict exists only in the mind of the disputants. Even in our century, when life is lived so much in watertight compartments, no one thinks of asking whether the painters of easel pictures work for self-expression or because they intend to sell their canvases. Nor, looking back, do we ask whether the Fra Angelico and his like worked because they were artists or because they were employed by the Church. In primitive societies, where there is no conscious division between intellectual, aesthetic, practical and religious activities, art belongs to them all and is simply a part of everyday life. To try to separate it out only reveals the folly of the over-analytical and unimaginative mind.

There is no question that most cave art served magical functions —in particular, the form known as sympathetic magic which depends upon the belief that similarity or relationship is identity, and that what is done to an image or part of a thing will affect the thing itself. Even in civilized lands people are still brought into court from time to time for making wax models of their enemies and melting them, or sticking them with pins.

Paleolithic art served sympathetic magic for the fulfilment of two great desires of the hunting people—for fertility in man and beast and for success in hunting. The first desire may be partly expressed in the very paintings and sculptures themselves—the artists were creating the game. It is expressed much more clearly in the portrayal of pregnant animals, as at Lascaux, in mating couples such as the lovely reindeer in Font de Gaume and the clay bison of Tuc d'Audubert, and above all in the emergence of the figures of the Mother Goddess. The second desire, the desire to kill, was served most obviously of all by the drawing of wounds, spears and darts on the flanks of the painted images. It takes a purely magical and non-aesthetic form at Montespan, where a rough clay dummy of a bear seems to have been furnished with the pelt and head of a real animal and frenziedly thrust with spears.

Yes, there is no doubt that cave art served the "practical" ends of magic. Yet this in no way lessens its greatness as art or the status of its creators as artists. From that time to this, there have been great numbers of hunting peoples living and practicing magic; yet none has had a representational art to approach theirs. The Bushmen, who come nearest to it, may have inherited some part of their tradition. The grisly relics at Montespan should themselves remind us that usually no attempt at realistic representation is thought necessary; symbolic designs or crude enactments supply the necessary magical identification. The few other peoples, like the Australians, who have made pictures in connection with hunting magic, have done so without inspiration or skill.

If, on the one hand, hunting magic is usually practiced without a noble, humane art such as the Paleolithic artists achieved, so, on the other, there is no doubt these artists often worked for the sheer enjoyment of creation. This is more evident in the small works than in the murals. It can perhaps be argued, though not very convincingly, that the carving of animals on spear-throwers may have been intended to give them added power as weapons of the chase. But surely no such magical purposes need be found for the innumerable little carvings and engraved sketches found in the cave dwellings? And what explanation save pleasure in the making and using of attractive objects can there be for the ibex drawn on a clay lamp from La Mouthe and the pretty fish palette?

One further element in the meaning of this art still remains to be considered—the religious. A number of cave drawings show men disguised as animals or with animal attributes. Some of these may merely be hunters, dressed up in order to stalk their prey; but many, such as the "imps" of Abri Mege, the masked grotesques of Combarelles and above all the famous Trois Frères "Sorcerer," certainly are not. They show men participating in animal life, not merely simulating it. The "Sorcerer," equally strange in style, form and feeling, is surely no human being at all but some spirit ancestor of man and beast such as survives in the concepts of modern totemism. That there were animal cults is further supported by the engraving from Raymonden, showing lines of human figures round a dismembered bison—possibly participants in some ritual communion meal —and by the comparable scene from La Madeleine, where a procession with bowed heads approaches a gigantic bison figure.

It seems that as these ancient hunters, with their heightening mental powers, began to feel themselves more and more cut off from the rest of nature, they yearned for reunion with it. And, because the whole of their lives were both actively and emotionally concentrated on the beautiful animals among which they lived, this desire for communion, for a *participation mystique,* went out towards them. For the tribe it probably found expression through dances and other ceremonies; for those few among them who had genius it found expression in their art.

A modern poet has said that "the poetic image shows the artist seeking to express unity with all that is and has been"; and this was as true of the first artists as of the latest. Various attempts have been made to suggest that the cave painters used dead beasts as their models, or that the sight of shadows on the wall suggested their imitation in paint. Such ideas are wholly misleading. Anyone with an understanding of the creative process must know that the artists who entered these dark caverns, so remote from the outer world, carried with them intense and emotionally charged images of the animals on which their lives were centered. The creative act, as in all true art, had already taken place in the imagination; the pigments, the graver, served only to give it material expression. All decorative and utilitarian magical functions apart, the element of communion with his animal subjects made the activity of the Paleolithic artist absolutely at one with the religious life of his society.

INTRODUCTION

Human history in the New World began with the migration of Upper Paleolithic hunters from northeastern Asia at a time very near the end of the Pleistocene, probably something on the order of 15,-000-20,000 years ago, or 18,000-13,000 B.C. At various time intervals there were land bridges connecting Siberia and Alaska as well as ice-free corridors in the far Northwest that would have facilitated the movement of animal herds and the hunters who preyed on them. Once they had entered the western plains, it was only a short time before most of the hemisphere was occupied. By eleven thousand years ago, or 9000 B.C., the ancestors of our modern Indians had reached Patagonia at the southernmost end of the Americas.

We do not know a great deal about these earliest Americans. None of their skeletal remains has ever been found, although we can assume that at this late date they must have been fully *sapiens* in type. The resemblance of present-day Indians to the peoples of northern Asia gives us a fair idea of what the Paleo-Indians must have looked like.

Furthermore, it is rather seldom that their actual settlements are located. Stone implements from this horizon occur as stray finds over most of the United States east of the Rockies, and, in a number of instances, mostly west of the Mississippi, these have been found in association with the carcasses of animals killed by the hunters, who were largely dependent upon extinct mammals such as mammoth, mastodon, bison, horse, camel, and giant ground sloth. Different groups of Paleo-Indians made their own distinctive types of lanceheads to which archaeologists have given names like "Clovis" and

"Folsom." In the following selection is described a typical "kill-site," where Clovis hunters ambushed and butchered a mammoth.

◇   ◇   ◇

Many of the evidences of America's oldest inhabitants are exposed during Nature's restless rearrangement of the solid matter of the earth's surface. What was once buried is again brought to view. An effective agent in this process is water. Laden with clay, silt or sand, it places a concealing mantle over whatever lies in its course during times of earth-building; in periods of earth-cutting, the same may be exposed. This was the case with the discovery of the Naco mammoth.

Greenbush Creek is a tributary of the San Pedro River, situated about a mile west of Naco, a little Arizona town which straddles the United States-Mexico border some ten miles southwest of Bisbee. This gravel-strewn channel, about 4,500 feet above sea level, is dry during most of the year but at times it becomes a rushing torrent which eats away at the bank. For some fifteen years Fred and Marc Navarrete, father and son who are residents of Naco, have been watching this channel for fossil remains which appeared from time to time. In August, 1951, after summer freshets had newly eroded the bank, they noticed that bones appeared in view. This encouraged them to dig in an attempt to salvage what appeared to be part of the skull of a large animal including teeth and tusk. In the course of this work they found near the skull a stone projectile point in an apparently undisturbed context. Additional digging soon revealed the left foreleg, scapula, humerus and ulna. Near the upper margin of the scapula, again in the undisturbed clay, a second projectile point came to light.

At this point the Navarretes realized that the find had great scientific value and they reported it at once to the Arizona State Museum. It is owing to their interest and understanding that this important find was preserved. In the spring of 1952 regular excavation was undertaken.

Excavation entails more than mere removal of objects from the earth. Inevitably there are problems which demand the assistance of a variety of specialists. In this case there was first the physical task of exposing the fragile bones without damage and of determining with

Emil Haury, "A Mammoth Hunt in Arizona." From *Archaeology*, VIII (1955), 51-55. Reprinted by permission of *Archaeology* and the author.

certainty that the man-made tools were contemporaneous with the bones. A paleontologist was needed, to determine precisely what kind of animal we had found; a geologist's knowledge was vital to the understanding of the age of the discovery. It would also be necessary to save clays for pollen analysis as an aid to dating, and charcoal, if present, for Carbon 14 analysis, the newest method for calculating age. Our first move, after learning the location of the bones and the nature of the matrix in which they occurred, was to strip the surrounding area of the covering of silt fallen from the arroyo bank and recently washed in by the creek. This exposed the clay in which the bones were encased and at the same time revealed the extent of the Navarretes' excavation. We could then be sure that we were digging in undisturbed ground. Next came the slow process of removing the clay from around the bones. Gradually the extent of the bone deposit was determined as well as the locality of greatest concentration of ribs and vertebrae, the area most likely to contain other projectile points.

The careful process described above had excellent results, for we discovered eight spear points in all. One was found near the base of the skull, one near the upper margin of the left shoulder blade, five among the ribs and vertebrae and one with position indeterminate. Although none of the eight points was imbedded in a bone, their positions were such as to leave no doubt that these were the weapons with which the mammoth was killed. Whether the spears were thrust or thrown we shall perhaps never know with certainty, yet the hazards of close-range thrusting at such a formidable creature would suggest that at least the first spears were thrown. Once it had been crippled, the animal could have been dispatched with effective jabs. We reconstruct the story in somewhat this manner: while drinking from a small stream the mammoth was surprised by one or more hunters, who brought it to earth with no less than eight well aimed spears. It fell on the sloping surface of a sand bar in or near the water's edge. The animal was defleshed on the spot and its hind quarters may have been carried away. After decomposition of the tissues remaining after the removal of the meat, some of the bones were displaced. No one bothered to pick up the spear points, which appear to have remained close to the places where they lodged on entering the body.

The exact identification of the animal was determined by careful study of the teeth. Though large, these are not the adult teeth, which were found unerupted in the jaw. This indicates that the animal was comparatively young, between twenty-five and sixty years of age. It is of the species *Mammuthus (Parelephas) columbi,* or Columbian Mammoth.

The spear points, although of various sizes, are all of the Clovis Fluted type, named after Clovis, New Mexico, where the form was first recognized. Similar spearheads have also been recovered among the bones of elephants in Nebraska, Colorado and Texas, which shows that the ancient elephant hunters wandered far afield. Those found at Naco are of two materials: dusky red and brown chert, and a dark gray felsite. The considerable range in the size of the points (5.8 cm. to 11.6 cm.) shows that the largest animals known to ancient hunters were not always hunted with only the largest tips on their spears.

We may visualize the sequence of events leading to the preservation of the bones somewhat as follows: within a few years of the slaughter the stream was dammed and what remained of the carcass then lay in a pond. (That this took place within a few years is indicated by the good preservation of the delicate parts of the bones.) The ponding provided the conditions for the formation of the clays which preserved the bones. Over the years the protective mantle of earth was deepened by successive flooding of the area. It may also be inferred that no one visited the site between the time of the "kill" and the disappearance of the bones under water; else the spear points, some of which must have lain in plain view, would most likely have been carried off.

This and other discoveries have proved that hunters in America killed and feasted upon animals which no longer exist. Exactly when this happened is difficult to determine. The age cannot be based on the kinds of animals killed because as yet we do not know either the exact time or the order of extinction. The climatic history preserved in the earth above the "kill" is, at present, our most reliable and widely used clue. Dr. Ernst Antevs, a leading specialist in this study, has dated the Naco find to a period between 11,000 and 10,000 years ago. Charcoal which was found in the clay near the mammoth bones is also expected to yield information about the date when it has been subjected to Carbon 14 analysis.

The San Pedro Valley has long been known as a fertile source of paleontological material, and it may be expected to continue to yield information about early man and his way of life.

V / THE NEOLITHIC REVOLUTION

INTRODUCTION

Plant and animal domestication, which initiated the so-called Neo-lithic level of culture, quite possibly ranks as the most significant discovery in the history of mankind. The inherent advantages of a food-producing economy are self-evident; man was now freed from complete dependence upon wild food resources and therefore less affected by natural fluctuations in the availability of these resources. By raising animals and easily-stored cereal grains, he no longer had to adapt himself so closely to seasonal variations in his environment. This direct control over the food supply also resulted in the production and accumulation of surpluses, which were to have important implications not only for future economic patterns, but for social and political organization as well. Agriculture, unlike most forms of food-collecting, fostered population growth and the establishment of relatively large and permanent settlements with more substantial dwellings. With a greater amount of leisure, more time could be spent in the elaboration of crafts, and eventually a portion of the population was able to devote its energies full time to activities other than those involved with obtaining food. Although true urban civilization, with bureaucratic government, spectacular architecture, public works, extensive commerce, and specialized classes of priests, rulers, artisans, and warriors, did not appear for some time, an agricultural economy was a precondition for all these changes.

We are not entirely certain of the exact circumstances under which the domestication of plants and animals began. A large share of the difficulty lies in the recognition of the earliest farming communities, since the first farmers probably still occupied caves or impermanent open-air settlements, had not yet developed new kinds of tools specifically suited to agricultural work, and continued to rely heavily upon wild foods for subsistence. An archaeologist excavating their sites often cannot ascertain whether they were agriculturists or not. Between about 9000 B. C. and 7000 B. C., a number of such groups inhabited Southwest Asia. These people not only engaged in hunting and fishing, but also harvested some sort of grasses with flint sickles and ground this into meal on stone mortars. We do not know if these grasses being reaped were wild or if they had been sown and cultivated as well. Animal bones are sometimes recovered, but one cannot always be sure one is dealing with stockbreeders since the skeletal remains of newly domesticated animals and those of their wild ancestors or relatives are nearly indistinguishable. However, in northern Iraq one site that belongs to this time period and that has a radiocarbon date of 8900 B. C. is said to have contained bones of domestic sheep.

Whoever first experimented with domestication must have had considerable familiarity with growth and reproduction in plants. We can infer from what we know of modern food-gatherers that women were responsible for the earliest cultivation. In modern food-gathering cultures, men usually hunt and fish while women collect edible roots, seeds, nuts, or berries as a supplement to the diet. Among prehistoric food-gatherers someone probably discovered that weeding out undesirable plants would promote better yields in the patches of wild root or seed plants that were being utilized. Once having some concept of growth cycles, these people struck on the idea of saving some seeds or shoots to start another crop in a more convenient location. As soon as someone began to select these from certain plants that were sturdier, larger, or more productive, domestication had begun. If we can judge from the division of labor among primitive horticulturists today, much of the cultivation probably was left to the women until such a time as it became the primary source of food, largely replacing game and fish.

With respect to animal domestication, it seems likely that hunters occasionally caught young animals that were brought home and tamed. It would take no great amount of mental gymnastics to see that keeping these animals and allowing them to breed in captivity was an easy means of storing meat until it was required. Nor were these incipient stockbreeders slow to recognize that the use of dairy products greatly increased the food value of their animals. Undoubtedly, people attempted to tame a variety of animals and found that only a few species were really responsive to this treatment. Almost all our common barnyard animals were domesticated before the dawn of recorded history, and one can add that turkeys were being raised by prehistoric American Indians and that chickens had already been domesticated from Southeast Asian jungle fowl. The same comment is true of cultivation, for virtually all important cereal grains, root crops, vegetables, and fruits were domesticated in prehistory. The exceptions are mostly either foods of secondary significance, like blueberries, or plants and trees yielding nonedible products of industrial value, such as rubber.

Nearly everyone looks to the eastern Mediterranean area that historians have long called the "Fertile Crescent" as the geographical region in which agriculture originated. This inverted crescent begins in the Nile Valley, sweeps up into northern Syria, and then spreads down the Tigris-Euphrates drainage system of Iraq to terminate in what was Mesopotamia. Other early centers of agriculture and civilization arose in northern China and the Indus Valley of West Pakistan. Of all these, Southwest Asia seems to take precedence in agricultural innovation, since the appearance of Neolithic communities in China and India-Pakistan, as well as in Egypt, was later in time and probably stimulated directly or indirectly by events in Southwest Asia. At this time, we have little or no archaeological proof concerning other areas of possibly independent agricultural development in Southeast Asia or northern Africa, although some favorable hypotheses have been advanced on their behalf by geographers, ethnologists, and botanists.

◇   ◇   ◇

As a revolution the introduction of a food-producing economy should affect the lives of all concerned, so as to be reflected in the population curve. Of course, no "vital statistics" have been recorded to prove that the expected increase of population did occur. But it is easy to see that it should. The community of food-gatherers had been restricted in size by the food supplies available—the actual number of game animals, fish, edible roots, and berries growing in its territory. No human effort could augment these supplies, whatever magicians might say. Indeed, improvements in the technique or intensification of hunting and collecting beyond a certain point would result in the progressive extermination of the game and an absolute diminution of supplies. And, in practice, hunting populations appear to be nicely adjusted to the resources at their disposal.

From V. Gordon Childe, *Man Makes Himself* (London: C. A. Watts & Co., Ltd., 1948). Reprinted by permission of C. A. Watts & Co., Ltd.

Cultivation at once breaks down the limits thus imposed. To increase the food supply it is only necessary to sow more seed, to bring more land under tillage. If there are more mouths to feed, there will also be more hands to till the fields.

Again, children become economically useful. To hunters children are liable to be a burden. They have to be nourished for years before they can begin to contribute to the family larder effectively. But quite young toddlers can help in weeding fields and scaring off birds or trespassing beasts. If there are sheep and cattle, boys and girls can mind them. *A priori*, then, the probability that the new economy was accompanied by an increase of population is very high. That population did really expand quite fast seems to be established by archaeology. Only so can we explain the apparent suddenness with which peasant communities sprang up in regions previously deserted or tenanted only by very sparse groups of collectors.

Round the lake that once filled the Fayum depression the number of Old Stone Age tools is certainly imposing. But they have to be spread over so many thousand years that the population they attest may be exiguous. Then, quite abruptly, the shore of a somewhat shrunken lake is found to be fringed with a chain of populous hamlets, all seemingly contemporary and devoted to farming. The Nile Valley from the First Cataract down to Cairo is quickly lined with a chain of flourishing peasant villages, all seeming to start about the same time and all developing steadily down to 3000 B. C. Or take the forest plains of northern Europe. After the Ice Age we find there scattered settlements of hunters and fishers along the coasts, on the shores of lagoons, and on sandy patches in the forest. The relics collected from such sites should probably be spread over a couple of thousand years, and so are only compatible with a tiny population. But then, within the space of a few centuries, Denmark first, and thereafter southern Sweden, north Germany, and Holland, become dotted with tombs built of gigantic stones. It must have taken a considerable force to build such burial-places, and in fact some contain as many as two hundred skeletons. The growth of the population must then have been rapid. It is true that in this case the first farmers, who were also the architects of the big stone graves, are supposed to have been immigrants. But as they are supposed to have come by boat from Spain round Orkney and across the North Sea, the actual immigrant population cannot have been very large. The multitude implied by the tombs must have resulted from the fecundity of a few immigrant families and that of the older hunters who had joined with these in exploiting the agricultural resources of the virgin north. Finally, the human skeletons assigned to the New Stone Age in Europe alone are several hundred times more numerous than those from the whole of the Old Stone Age. Yet the New Stone Age in Europe lasted at the outside two thousand years— less than one hundredth of the time assigned to the Old!

In practically all the oldest food-producing settlements examined by archaeologists in Europe, Hither Asia, and North Africa, the basic industry is mixed farming; in addition to the cultivation of cereals, animals are bred for food. This economy is characteristic of the "Neolithic" stage wherever such exist. The food animals kept were not very varied: horned cattle, sheep, goats, and swine. Comparatively few species—fowls are the most important—have been added to the farmyards in subsequent periods or other countries. Horned cattle require rather rich grass, but can live on well-watered steppes, in naturally irrigated valleys, and even in forests that are not too dense. Pigs like swamps or woodlands; sheep and goats can thrive under dry, though not absolutely desert, conditions, and both are at home in hilly and mountainous country. Wild goats probably once ranged all along the mountains that divide Eurasia lengthwise, perhaps from the Pyrenees, or at least from the Balkans eastward to the Himalaya. Wild sheep lived along the same chains, but of three distinct varieties. The mouflon survives in the Mediterranean islands and the hill country of Hither Asia from Turkey to western Persia; east of the mouflon, in Turkestan, Afghanistan, and the Punjab, is the home of the urial; still farther east, in the mountains of central Asia, lives the argal. In Africa, no wild sheep is known. The oldest Egytpian sheep belong to the urial stock, as do the oldest European flocks; but the mouflon is represented side by side with the urial on early monuments from Mesopotamia. The reader will note that ancestors of our farmyard animals lived wild in most of the regions that seem likely to have comprised the cradle of grain-growing. But the absence of wild sheep from Africa makes Egypt unlikely as a starting point of mixing farming.

Hunters today, and doubtless in prehistoric times, have been accustomed to make pets of young wild animals for ritual ends or just for fun. Man has allowed the dog to frequent his camp in return for the offal of his prey and refuse from his feasts. Under the conditions of incipient desiccation the cultivator has the chance of attaching to his ménage not only isolated young beasts, but the remnants of complete flocks or herds, comprising animals of both sexes and all ages. If he just realizes the advantage of having a group of such half-tamed beasts hanging round the fringes of his settlement as a reserve of game easily caught, he will be on the way to domestication.

Next he must exercise restraint and discrimination in using this reserve of meat. He must refrain from frightening the beasts unnecessarily or killing the youngest and tamest. Once he begins to kill only the shyest and least amenable bulls or rams, he will have started selective breeding, eliminating untractable brutes, and consequently favoring the more docile. But he must also use his new opportunities of studying the life of the beasts at close range. He will thus learn about the processes of reproduction, the animals' needs of food and water. He must act upon his knowledge. Instead of merely driving the herd away when the time comes round for sowing his plots again, he must follow the beasts, guide them to suitable pastures and water, and continue to ward off predatory carnivora. It can thus be imagined how with lapse of time a flock or a herd should have been bred that was not only tame, but actually dependent upon man.

That result could happen only provided the peculiar climatic conditions continued long enough, and suitable animals were haunting human settlements. No doubt experiments were tried with various species; herds of antelopes and gazelles were kept by the Egyptians about 3000 B. C. These and other unknown experiments were fruitless. Luckily, cattle, sheep, goats, and pigs were included in the wild fauna of the desiccated regions in Asia. These did become firmly attached to man and ready to follow him.

At first the tame or domesticated beast would presumably be regarded only as a potential source of meat, an easily accessible sort of game. Other uses would be discovered later. It might be noticed that crops flourished best on plots that had been grazed over. Ultimately the value of dung as a fertilizer would be realized. The process of milking can only have been discovered when men had had ample opportunity of studying at close quarters the suckling of calves and lambs and kids. But once the trick was grasped, milk would become a second staple. It could be obtained without killing the beast, without touching your capital. Selection would again be applied. The best milkers would be spared, and their young reared in preference to other calves, lambs, or kids. Still later the hair of sheep or goats would win appreciation. It could be treated by processes, perhaps originally applied to plant fibers, and woven into cloth or else beaten into felt. Wool is entirely the artificial product of selective breeding. On wild sheep it is merely a down between the hairs. It was still unknown to the Egyptians even after 3000 B.C. But in Mesopotamia sheep were being bred for their wool before that date. The harnessing of animals to bear burdens or draw plows and vehicles is a late adaptation, and will be considered among the steps leading up to the second [urban] revolution in human economy.

The minimal characteristics of simple cultivation have already been considered. But these must now be pictured as combined with stock-breeding if we are to understand the basic economy revealed in Neolithic settlements in North Africa, Hither Asia, and Europe. If the number of animals kept remains quite small, the account already given will hold good, the animals will be put to graze on the stubble after the harvest and at other seasons on natural pastures round the settlement. Beyond telling off a few youths to look after the herd, the communal economy can be left as already described. But as soon as the flocks exceed a low limit, special provision may have to be made for them. Trees and scrub may be burned off to make room for grass. In a river valley it may be thought worthwhile to clear or irrigate special meadows to serve as pasture for cattle. Crops may be deliberately grown, harvested, and conserved to serve exclusively as fodder. Or the animals may be driven far afield to find pastures in the dry season. In Mediterranean lands, Persia, and Asia Minor there is good summer grazing on the hills which in winter are snow-clad. And so sheep and cattle are driven up to hill pastures in the spring. And now a regular company of the village's inhabitants must accompany the herds to ward off wild beasts, to milk the cows and ewes. The herders must generally take with them supplies of grain and other equipment. In some cases the fraction of the community that migrate with their gear to the summer pastures is quite small. But in hot and dry countries, like Persia, parts of the eastern Sudan, and in the northwestern Himalayas, the bulk of the community abandons its village in the stifling valley and accompanies the herds to the cooler hills. Only a few stay behind to look after the fields and dwellings.

From this it is no far cry to a purely pastoral economy in which cultivation plays a negligible role. Pure pastoral nomadism is familiar, and is illustrated by several peoples in the Old World; the Bedouin of Arabia and Mongolian tribes of central Asia are the best-known examples. How old such a mode of life may be is uncertain. Pastoralists are not likely to leave many vestiges by which the archaeologist could recognize their presence. They tend to use vessels of leather and basketry instead of pots, to live in tents instead of in excavated shelters or huts supported by stout timber posts or walls of stone or brick. Leather vessels and baskets have as a rule no chance of surviving; tents need not even leave deep post holes to mark where they once stood. (Though wood decays, modern archaeology can recognize the hole made by a post five thousand years ago.)

The failure to recognize prehistoric settlement sites or groups of relics belonging to pure pastoralists is not in itself any proof that such did not exist. To that extent the postulate of the "historical school," that pure pastoralism and pure hoe-culture were originally practiced independently by separate peoples and that mixed farming resulted from their subsequent fusion, is irrefutable. Yet Forde has recently emphasized the instability of pure pastoralism. Many typical pastoral tribes today, like the patriarchs in Genesis, actually cultivate grain, though in an incidental and rather casual manner. If they grow no grain themselves, pastoral nomads are almost always economically dependent upon settled peasant villages. The cultivators may be tributaries or serfs to the pastoralists, but they are essential to their subsistence.

Whatever its origin, stock-breeding gave man control over his own food supply in the same way as cultivation did. In mixed farming it becomes an equal partner in the food-producing economy. But just as the term "cultivation" covers many distinct modes of gaining a livelihood, so the single phrase "mixed farming" marks an equal disparity and diversity. The several different modes of cultivation may be combined in varying degrees with distinct attitudes to the livestock. The diversity of the permutations and combinations has just been suggested. The multiplicity of concrete applications of the food-producing economy must never be forgotten.

It must be remembered, too, that food-production does not at once supersede food-gathering. If today hunting is only a ritual sport and game is a luxury for the rich, fishing is still a great industry, contributing directly to everybody's diet. At first hunting, fowling, fishing, the collection of fruits, snails, and grubs continued to be essential activities in the food quest of any food-producing group. Grain and milk began as mere supplements to a diet of game, fish, berries, nuts, and ants' eggs. Probably at first cultivation was an incidental activity of the women while their lords were engaged in the really serious business of the chase. Only slowly did it win the status of an independent and ultimately predominant industry. When the archaeological record first reveals Neolithic communities in Egypt and Iran, survivals from the food-gathering régime clearly stand on an equal footing with grain-growing and stock-breeding.

Only subsequently does their economic importance decline. After the second revolution, hunting and fowling have become, as with us, ritual sports, or else, like fishing, specialized industries practiced by groups within the community or by independent societies, economically dependent upon an agricultural civilization.

Two other aspects of the simple food-producing economy deserve attention. In the first place, food-production, even in its simplest form, provides an opportunity and a motive for the accumulation of a surplus. A crop must not be consumed as soon as it is reaped. The grains must be conserved and eked out so as to last till the next harvest, for a whole year. And a proportion of every crop must be set aside for seed. The conservation is easy. But it means on the one hand forethought and thrift, on the other receptacles for storage. These are quite as essential as, and may actually be more elaborate than, dwellings. In the Neolithic villages of the Fayum, perhaps the oldest of their kind, excavated silos, lined with straw basketry or matting, are the most substantial constructions that have survived.

Again, livestock that has been laboriously carried over the dry season must not be indiscriminately slaughtered and devoured. The young cows and ewes at least must be spared and reared to provide milk and to augment the herd or flock. Once these ideas have been driven home, the production and accumulation of a surplus are much easier for food-producers than for food gatherers. The yield of crops and of herds soon outstrips the immediate needs of the community. The storage of grain, the conservation of live meat "on the hoof" is much simpler, especially in a warm climate, than the preservation of stocks of slaughtered game. The surplus thus gathered will help to tide the community over bad seasons; it will form a reserve against droughts and crop failures. It will serve to support a growing population. Ultimately it may constitute a basis for rudimentary trade, and so pave the way to a second revolution.

Secondly, the economy is entirely self-sufficing. The simple food-producing community is not dependent for any necessity of life on imports obtained by barter or exchange from another group. It produces and collects all the food it needs. It relies on raw materials available in its immediate vicinity for the simple equipment it demands. Its constituent members or households manufacture the requisite implements, utensils, and weapons.

This economic self-sufficiency does not necessarily spell isolation. The variations in the simple food-producing economy already indicated, the simultaneous pursuit of several methods of obtaining nourishment by different groups, are liable to bring the several communities concerned into mutual contact. Driving their flocks to summer pastures, the herdsmen from one village are likely to meet their counterparts from another. On hunting expeditions across the desert, huntsmen from one oasis may cross parties from another. In such ways the isolation of each community is liable to be broken down. Far from being a scattering of discrete units, the Neolithic world should be viewed as a continuous chain of communities. Each would be linked to its neighbors on either side by recurrent, if infrequent and irregular, contacts. . . .

However, all the groups of simple food-producers recognized by archaeology are distinguished from one another by very marked differences. Archaeologists divide them into a bewildering variety of "cultures." Each has its own distinctive types of tools, vessels, weapons, and ornaments, its own peculiar art and burial rites. Even the applications of the basic economy differ from group to group. Nomadic garden-culture was, for instance, the rule in western Europe, on the loess lands of central Europe, in the Ukraine, and in western China—all temperate regions. In Crete or Thessaly even the oldest settlements seem relatively permanent. Again, in western Europe the breeding of cattle, sheep, and swine, and hunting were at least on an equal footing with grain-growing. On the central European loess domestic animals seem to have played at first a minor role in the food supply, and game an altogether negligible one. The Neolithic Chinese kept only pigs.

Among the Neolithic Eygptians at Tasa cattle and sheep bones were found in plenty, but no remains of pig. That animal was, however, plentiful in the contemporary settlements in the Fayum and on the Delta's edge. Again the grains grown differ—emmer wheat in Egypt, Assyria, western and Northern Europe, dinkel in the Danube basin, bread-wheat perhaps in Syria and Turkestan. Thus there is no such thing as a Neolithic civilization. Various human groups of different racial composition, living under diverse conditions of climate and soil, have adopted the same ground ideas and adapted them differently to their several environments.

The differences which so clearly separate Neolithic cultures are not surprising in view of the distinctive character of the economy, the self-sufficiency of each community. Because each group was economically independent of any neighbors, it could remain isolated from them. And in such isolation each group could work out its own arts and crafts, its own styles and institutions independent of the rest. Only the most bigoted evolutionist will contend that these independent developments would converge everywhere to like results.

The reverse may be actually observed. If one studies in detail several closely allied Neolithic groups—on the central European loess, for example—one notices a continual divergence, the multiplication of individualized groups each differing from one another ever more pronouncedly in the fashionable shape for vases, the style of their decoration, and so on.

Nevertheless, the possible isolation was never actually realized—perhaps, indeed, complete economic self-sufficiency was nowhere attained. Everywhere intercourse between adjacent groups is attested to the archaeologist by an interchange of objects. Such might result from accidental contacts between herdsmen and hunters, such as we have anticipated, from formal visits, from the practice of seeking a wife outside one's own village (exogamy), and so on. It might lead up to a sort of irregular trade through which objects might travel great distances. So to Neolithic settlements on the Fayum lake shells were brought both from the Mediterranean and the Red Sea. Bracelets made from the shell of a Mediterranean mussel, *Spondylus gaederopi,* have been found in Neolithic graves even in Bohemia and south Germany.

The point is that such trade was not an integral part of the community's economic life; the articles it brought were in some sense luxuries, non-essentials. Yet the intercourse thus attested was of vital importance to human progress; it provided channels whereby ideas from one society might reach another, whereby foreign materials might be compared, whereby, in fact, culture itself might be diffused. Indeed, "Neolithic civilization" in part owes its expansion to the prior existence amongst still sparser hunting communities of a rudimentary web of intercourse.

In exceptional cases communication between separate groups of the kind here envisaged might lead to more regular "trade" and to intercommunal specialization even within the framework of the Neolithic economy. In England, Belgium, and France archaeologists have discovered Neolithic flint mines. The miners probably cultivated plants and bred cattle in the intervals of mining. But it is quite certain that they were not producing for themselves alone, but exporting their flints to a wider market. Nevertheless, where seas, forests, or wooded mountains intervened, intercourse in Neolithic times must generally have been very infrequent and the percolation of ideas exceedingly slow. Only in the arid zone round the Mediterranean and east thereof was intercourse at all rapid or extensive.

Thus "Neolithic times" may mean anything between 6000 B.C. and A.D. 1800. "Neolithic civilization" is a dangerous term applicable to a huge variety of cultural groups, all more or less on the same economic plane. . . .

In the later part of the Old Stone Age axe-like tools seem to have been unknown. The ground stone celt does not seem to derive directly from the "hand axe" of flaked stone or flint current earlier in the Old Stone Age. The essence of the Neolithic tool is that its edge is sharpened by grinding. The new technique might be suggested by effects observed on stone rubbers used for grinding grains on other stones. Or perhaps for digging up the garden plots a split pebble was lashed on to the end of a stick to make a sort of hoe; then the end of the pebble might be rubbed sharp by friction with sandy soil. But, though Neolithic celts are almost invariably found in the oldest settlements of simple food-producers, it is not certain that the implement is really a result of the new economy. Axe-like tools are found, for instance, on the Baltic, long before there are any indications of farming. The models there seem to be provided by implements of bone and antler, also sharpened by polishing. Ground stone axes and adzes were certainly used by some denizens of the north European forest who still bred no animals for food and cultivated no plants. And outside Europe many typical food-gatherers, including even the aborigines of Australia, used ground stone axes. On the other hand, the Natufians of Palestine, who certainly reaped something, presumably a cereal, with sickles, possessed no axes. The ground stone celt is not therefore an infallible sign of the Neolithic economy in the sense here used of self-sufficing food production.

Still, wherever it arose, the ground stone celt provided a tough implement and a resistant edge that would not be chipped or blunted by a few blows. It enabled man to hew and to shape timber. Carpentry could begin. Plows, wheels, plank-boats, wooden houses all require axes and adzes for their manufacture. The invention of the ground stone celt was an essential precondition for these later achievements.

The preparation and storage of cereal foods may be supposed to have put a premium upon vessels which would at once stand heat and hold liquids. A universal feature of Neolithic communities seems to have been the manufacture of pots. (Such were not, however, used by the Natufians of Palestine.) Pottery may, indeed, have been discovered before the rise of the food-producing economy. It might have originated in the accidental burning of a basket plastered with clay to make it water-tight. A couple of small fragments allegedly found in an Old Stone Age layer in Kenya suggest this possibility. But it is only in Neolithic times that pot-making is attested on a large scale; a Neolithic site is generally strewn with fragments of broken pottery.

The new industry has great significance for human thought and for the beginning of science. Pot-making is perhaps the earliest conscious utilization by man of a chemical change. The essence of the process is the expulsion by heat of some molecules of water (termed the "water of constitution") from the hydrated silicate of aluminum which is the chemist's name for potter's clay. A lump of clay when wet is completely plastic; it will disintegrate in excess of water and crumble to powder if dried. When the "water of constitution," chemically combined in it, is expelled rather above 600° C. the material loses its plasticity altogether; the whole lump solidifies, and will keep its shape wet or dry unless deliberately and laboriously broken up by crushing or pounding. The essence of the potter's craft is that she can mold a piece of clay into any shape she desires and then give that shape permanence by "firing" (i.e., heating to over 600° C.).

To early man this change in the quality of the material must have seemed a sort of magic transubstantiation—the conversion of mud or dust into stone. It may have prompted some philosophical questions as to the meaning of substance and sameness. How is the plastic clay the same substance as the hard but brittle earthenware? The pot you put into the fire has much the same shape as what you draw out, but the color has changed and the texture is quite different.

The discovery of pottery consisted essentially in finding out how to control and utilize the chemical change just mentioned. But, like all other discoveries, its practical application involves others. To be able to mold your clay you must wet it; but if you put your damp plastic pot straight into the fire, it will crack. The water, added to the clay to make it plastic, must be dried out gently in the sun or near the fire, before the vessel can be baked. Again, the clay has to be selected and prepared. If it contains too large grits, it will not model easily nor yield a handsome or serviceable pot; some process of washing must be devised to eliminate coarse material. On the other hand, if the clay contains no grit, it will stick to the fingers in molding and crack in firing. To avoid this danger some gritty material—sand, powdered stone or shell, chopped straw, what is termed a "temper"—must be added.

In the process of firing, the clay changes not only its physical consistency, but also its color. The latter change is determined partly by chemical impurities in the material, partly by the process of firing.

Most clays contain some iron oxide. If the air has free access to the pot while it is hot, the vessel will come out with a reddish hue because the iron will be oxidized to form the red ferric oxide. But if the pot be surrounded during firing with glowing charcoal and the gases given off during imperfect combustion, the iron salts will be reduced, and the product will be gray, because ferroso-ferric oxide is black. A dark color may also be produced by free carbon in the clay. That may be derived from the charring of vegetable or organic impurities in the raw material, or from soot from the fire soaking into the pores of the red-hot earthenware, or from fats or dung deliberately applied to the vase surface while it is still hot. Man had to learn to control such changes as these and to utilize them to enhance the beauty of the vessel.

At first, local conditions, the sort of clay and fuel available on the spot, would be allowed to determine the color of the pot. Average clays, burned in the smoky brushwood fires of well-watered regions, yield black or dirty gray vessels. Under rather drier climates reds and brown can be produced. The hot fires made from thorny Mediterranean or desert plants easily yield pale buff, pinkish, or greenish wares. Subsequently the potter learns how to produce such effects at will or to enhance them for the embellishment of the vessel. She might, for instance, cover the vase's surface with a thin layer—a "slip" or wash—of selected clay, rich in iron oxides, in order to produce a good red ware. She might even apply such specially prepared clays with a brush so as to outline painted patterns. It must be remembered that the effect of color painted on an unfired vessel is quite different from that of the final product. Vase-painting is no simple art; the artist has to forecast in advance what the fired pot is going to look like. The feat was early achieved in Hither Asia. It was a long time before painted pottery could be manufactured in temperate regions where the natural fuel gave a smoky flame.

There the light ground needed to show up painted decoration could only be achieved with the aid of a further invention—a built oven or kiln in which the vases can be raised to 900° or 1000° C., and yet kept out of contact with the flames. Such a device is not attested for the earliest Neolithic communities; it does not reach central or western Europe till the Iron Age.

Thus the potter's craft, even in its crudest and most generalized form, was already complex. It involved an appreciation of a number of distinct processes, the application of a whole constellation of discoveries. Only a few of these have been even mentioned. At the risk of boring the reader, we must note one more. The shaping of the pot itself is not so easy as it sounds. Quite small vessels can, of course, be kneaded and molded, mud-pie fashion, out of a lump of clay. Or a coating of clay can be spread over an open basket or a half-gourd; when it has dried, the form can be removed, and you have an open dish or platter ready for firing.

But if anything larger is desired, or a vessel with a narrow neck like a bottle or jug, such elementary processes no longer suffice: the vessel must be built up. In Neolithic Europe and Asia this was generally done by the ring method; after the base had been molded, rings of clay of the desired diameter were prepared. One was attached to the base and then another set on the top edge of this, and so on. It is a slow process. The rings must be fairly wet and plastic when they are put on. But as soon as one ring is in place, you must pause and let it dry and harden—but not too much—before adding the next story. The mere construction of a large pot may take several days.

The constructive character of the potter's craft reacted on human thought. Building up a pot was a supreme instance of creation by man. The lump of clay was perfectly plastic; man could mold it as he would. In making a tool of stone or bone he was always limited by the shape and size of the original material; he could only take bits away from it. No such limitations restrict the activity of the potter. She can form her lump as she wishes; she can go on adding to it without any doubts as to the solidity of the joins. In thinking of "creation," the free activity of the potter in "making form where there was no form" constantly recurs to man's mind; the similes in the Bible taken from the potter's craft illustrate the point.

In practice the potter's freedom to create was not at first fully utilized. Fancy cannot work in a vacuum. What it creates must be like something already known. Moreover, pots were generally made by women and for women, and women are particularly suspicious of radical innovations. So the earliest pots are obvious imitations of familiar vessels made from other materials—from gourds, from bladders, membranes, and skins, from basketry and wickerwork, or even from human skulls. To enhance the resemblance, the grass sling in which a gourd, like a modern Chianti flask, was carried, the stitching of the "wine-skin," or the interlacing fibers of the basket were often imitated by patterns, incised or painted on the pot. Thus the vessel in the fresh material came to look less new-fangled and outlandish to the prudent housewife!

Among the remains of the earliest Neolithic villages of Egypt and Hither Asia we find the first indications of a textile industry. Manufactured garments, woven out of linen, or later wool, begin to compete with dressed skins or skirts of leaves as protection against cold and sun. For this to be possible another complex of discoveries and inventions is requisite, a further body of scientific knowledge must be practically applied. In the first place, a suitable material was needed, a fibrous substance that would yield long threads. The Neolithic villagers on the Fayum lake were already using flax. They must have selected this from all other plants and begun to cultivate it deliberately in addition to growing cereals. Another variety of flax may have been discovered and grown in Asia. A local European flax was cultivated and utilized in Switzerland in Neolithic times.

Other materials must have been tried. Cotton was certainly being grown in the Indus Valley soon after 3000 B.C. Wool, as already noted, was used in Mesopotamia about the same time. Before wool-bearing sheep had been produced by selective breeding, the hairs of sheep and goats may have served for the production of a sort of cloth, since hair can be woven. A textile industry thus not only requires the knowledge of special substances like flax, cotton, and wool, but also the breeding of special animals and the cultivation of particular plants.

Among the prerequisite inventions a device for spinning is important. The little discs of stone or pottery, termed whorls, that served to weight the end of a spindle, like miniature flywheels, generally constitute the sole tangible proof of the existence of a textile industry that an archaeologist can hope to find. Only very exceptional conditions can preserve actual textile products or the wooden implements used in their production.

Of these the most essential is a loom. It is, indeed, possible to produce a sort of cloth with the aid of a frame by a sort of glorified plaiting process similar to that employed in making mats. Blankets of dogs' hair were actually produced in this way by food-gathering tribes on the northwest coast of Canada last century. But in the Old World a true loom goes back to Neolithic times. Now a loom is quite an elaborate piece of machinery—much too elaborate to be described here. Its use is no less complicated. The invention of the loom was one of the great triumphs of human ingenuity. Its inventors are nameless, but they made an essential contribution to the capital stock of human knowledge, an application of science that only to the unthinking seems too trivial to deserve the name.

All the foregoing industries require for their exercise a technical skill that can only be acquired by training and practice. Yet all were household crafts. In our hypothetical Neolithic stage there would be no specialization of labor—at most a division of work between the sexes. And that system can still be seen at work today. Among hoe-cultivators the women generally till the fields, build up and fire the pots, spin, and weave; men look after animals, hunt and fish, clear the plots for cultivation, and act as carpenters, preparing their own tools and weapons. But, of course, to such a generalization there are many exceptions: among the Yoruba, for instance, weaving is in the hands of men.

All the industries named, from garden culture to weaving, have been rendered possible only by the accumulation of experience and the application of deductions therefrom. Each and all repose on practical science. Moreover, the exercise of each craft is throughout regulated and directed by a constantly expanding body of practical science. The appropriate lore is handed on from parent to child for generation after generation. The cultivator, for instance, must know in practice what soil it is most profitable to till, when to break up the ground, how to distinguish young grain shoots from sprouting weeds, and a host of other details. The young potter must learn to find and choose proper clay, how to clean it, with what proportion of water and grit it should be mixed, and so on.

Thus there grows up to be handed on a great body of craft lore— snippets of botany, geology, and chemistry, one might say. If we may judge from the procedure of modern barbarians, the legitimate de-ductions from experience are inextricably mixed up with what we should call useless magic. Each operation of every craft must be accompanied by the proper spells and the prescribed ritual acts. All this body of rules, practical and magical, forms part of the craft tradition. It is handed on from parent to child by example and by precept. The daughter helps her mother at making pots, watches her closely, imitates her, and receives from her lips oral directions, warn-ings, and advice. The applied sciences of Neolithic times were handed on by what today we should call a system of apprenticeship.

The Neolithic crafts have been presented as household industries. Yet the craft traditions are not individual, but collective traditions. The experience and wisdom of all the community's members are constantly being pooled. In a modern African village the housewife does not retire into seclusion in order to build up and fire her pots. All the women of the village work together, chatting and comparing notes; they even help one another. The occupation is public; its rules are the result of communal experience. And so in prehistoric times all the pots from a given Neolithic village exhibit a monotonous uniformity. They bear the stamp of a strong collective tradition rather than of individuality.[1]

And the Neolithic economy as a whole cannot exist without co-operative effort. The heavier labor of clearing patches in a forest or draining a marsh must be a collective undertaking. The digging of drains, the defense of the settlement against wild beasts or floods, must again be communal responsibilities. The dwellings in Neolithic villages both in Egypt and in western Europe have been proved to be arranged in a regular order, not scattered about indiscriminately. All this implies some social organization to coordinate and control the communal activities. What that organization was we can never know exactly. One assertion seems plausible.

The effective unit of social organization in pure Neolithic times was generally very small. A typical Thessalian village, rather advanced in the period, covered an area of 100 by 45 meters, or just over one acre! Several Neolithic cemeteries have been fully explored in central Europe. None contained more than twenty graves. (Of course, we do not know how long the settlement was occupied nor how many generations are represented in each cemetery.) Among modern representatives of garden-cultivation a tendency for the village to break up has been noted by ethnographers. Some of the young men hive off with their wives and start a new village of their own. They like the freedom of their new settlement, in which they are exempt from the authority and oversight of their elders. Then, founding a new village with plots of virgin jungle close to the dwellings saves long walks to the gardens, such as become necessary when the original village is populous and the nearest land has already been used up. On the whole the separation would be convenient—provided, of course, there was land available. In Neolithic times there was as yet no shortage.

Undoubtedly the cooperative activities involved in "Neolithic" life found outward expression in social and political institutions. Undoubtedly such institutions were consolidated and reinforced by magico-religious sanctions, by a more or less coherent system of beliefs and superstitions, by what Marxists would call an ideology. The new forces controlled by man as the result of the Neolithic revolution and the knowledge gained and applied in the exercise of the new crafts must have reacted upon man's outlook. They must

[1] Yet certain "Neolithic" communities today recognize the proprietary rights of individuals or families to particular patterns, ceremonies, or processes.

have modified his institutions and his religion. But precisely what form Neolithic institutions and beliefs assumed is unknowable. . . .

The "Neolithic revolution" was not a catastrophe, but a process. Its several stages were doubtless modifying the social institutions and magico-religious ideas of food-gatherers and hunters. But it would be long before any new system or systems, more appropriate to the nascent economy, became firmly established. Ere then the second revolution may already have been beginning. It was perhaps the very absence of rigid ideologies and deeply-rooted institutions that permitted the rapid progress from self-sufficing villages to industrial and commercial cities in less than 2000 years.

Firmly entrenched institutions, passionately held superstitions, are notoriously inimical to social change and the scientific advances that make it necessary. And the force of such reaction in a community seems to be inversely proportional to the community's economic security. A group always on the brink of starvation dare not risk change. The least deviation from the traditional procedures that have been found to yield the essential modicum of subsistence may imperil the whole group. It would be just as dangerous to antagonize the mysterious magic powers that control the weather by omitting a rite or a sacrifice as to omit poisoning the arrowhead that is to slay an elephant.

Now, even after the first revolution, life remained very precarious for the little group of self-sufficing peasants. A drought, a hailstorm, a blight might mean famine. Such peasants had no world market to draw upon, so that deficiencies of crops in one area could be compensated by a surplus in another. They had still only a limited variety of sources of food. All their several crops, their herds, and their game might easily be affected by the same catastrophe. The reserves in store were never large. A self-sufficing peasant community is inevitably fully conscious of its immediate dependence on the powers that bring rain and sunshine, thunder and hurricane. But these act capriciously and terribly. At all costs they must be compelled, cajoled, or conciliated.

Now, once you can make yourself believe that you have found a system of magic to achieve that compulsion, or a ritual to ensure that conciliation, the belief becomes a solace in the terrors of life that one dare not surrender. Had such magics and rituals been firmly established, they would surely have retarded the spread of the second revolution. After it, firmly rooted beliefs—for instance, in the efficacy of astrology and the potency of divine kings and ancestral spirits—did impede the growth of true science and the establishment of an inter-urban international economy. But perhaps the first revolution was still just sapping confidence in the necessity of hunters' magic and its political consequences when the disturbing ideas and discoveries heralding the second revolution were emerging. Perhaps any new system of organization and belief, adapted to the Neolithic economy, had not become established and rooted when the economy itself began to dissolve in the Orient.

Nevertheless, certain hints are available as to institutions that did or did not subsist in Neolithic times. Sometimes they seem to have reacted upon the form taken by the second revolution. That many institutions were taken over from the older order is only natural. In the Nile Valley there is indirect evidence of the survival of a system of totemic clans. The later Neolithic villages seem to have been the settlements belonging to such clans. When in historical times the villages became the capitals of parishes (nomes), they bore names like Elephantine and Falcontown (Hierakonpolis), taken apparently from the totem of the localized clan, the elephant and the falcon. The standards of the parishes were clan emblems, and even in prehistoric times such emblems figure upon the vases. Such a clan system is not uncommon among simple food-producers today, and may be a genuine survival from Neolithic times. But that all Neolithic communities were organized as totemic clans cannot be asserted.

Of chieftainship there is no definite evidence in early Neolithic cemeteries or villages. There are, that is to say, no outstandingly wealthy graves, evidently belonging to a person of rank, and no dwellings that could pass for palaces. The great stone graves of western and northern Europe which do look princely belong to a time when ideas proper to the second revolution were being diffused, and they are probably inspired thereby. Houses larger than the normal have been noted in some Neolithic villages in Europe, but they may be communal lodges or clubs, like the bachelors' houses of the Pacific Islanders, rather than princely residences. Nor is there unambiguous evidence of warfare. Weapons are certainly often found in Neolithic graves and settlements. But were they arms of war or merely implements of the chase? Woman's increasing share in the provision of food for the community may have raised also the social status of the sex. But that too is uncertain.

As to the magico-religious notions that held Neolithic communities together, a few guesses may be hazarded. The tendance of the dead, going far back into the Old Stone Age, may have assumed a deeper significance in the new. In the case of several Neolithic groups, indeed, no burials have been discovered. But generally the dead were carefully interred in built or excavated graves, either grouped in cemeteries near the settlement or dug close to the individual dwellings. The dead are normally provided with utensils or weapons, vases of food and drink, and toilet articles. In prehistoric Egypt pictures of animals and objects are painted on the funerary vases. They presumably had the same magic significance as the cave painting and rock carvings of Old Stone Age hunters. In historical times they were transferred to the walls of the tomb, and then attached texts show that they were really designed to insure to the dead the continued enjoyment of the services they depict.

Such tendance denotes an attitude to the ancestral spirits that goes back to far older periods. But now the earth in which the ancestors' remains lie buried is seen as the soil from which the community's food supply magically springs each year. The ancestral spirits must surely be regarded as assisting in the crops' germination.

Fertility cults, magic rites to assist or compel the forces of reproduction, may have become more prominent than ever in Neolithic times. Small figurines of women, carved in stone or ivory, with the sexual characters well marked, have been noted in camps of the Old Stone Age. But similar figures, now generally modeled in clay, are very common in Neolithic settlements and graves. They are often termed "Mother Goddesses." Was the earth from whose womb the young grain sprouts really conceived in the likeness of a woman with whose generative functions man is certainly familiar?

The early Oriental civilizations periodically celebrated with great pomp a "sacred marriage," the nuptial union of a "king" and a "queen," who on this occasion represented divinities. Their union not only symbolized, but also magically insured and compelled, the fertilization of the earth, that she might bring forth her fruits in due season. But the seed must die and be buried before it can sprout and multiply. A human representative of the grain, a "corn king," was once slain and buried. His place was taken by a young successor who should stand for the growing crops till he too must lie like the seed in the ground. These magical rites, these dramatic representations of the death and rebirth of the grain, were often mitigated in practice by historical times. But they can be discerned behind many early myths, and in Neolithic times may have been observed literally. Yet they might pave the way to political power. The "corn king" may claim by magic to have attained immortality. Then he is a secular king, too, entitled to the dignity of a god.

Finally, cultivation may have required a closer observation of the seasons, a more accurate division of time, the year. Agricultural operations are essentially seasonal, and their success is largely dependent upon the time of their performance. But the proper season is determined by the sun, not by the moon's phases, which provide a calendar for hunters. In northerly latitudes the changes in the sun's path between the solstices are conspicuous enough to provide clues as to the seasons. The observation of such clues would emphasize the sun's role as ruler of the seasons and guarantee his divinity.

But near the tropics the sun's movement is less striking. There the stars, always visible in those cloudless skies, provide a more obvious means of determining and dividing the solar year. You note that certain stars of constellations take up a significant position in the sky at the time when experience suggests you should plant your corps, others when you may expect rain to ripen them. By so using the stars as guides, men may have come to the belief that they actually influenced terrestrial affairs. You confuse connection in time with casual connection. Because the star Sirius is seen on the horizon at dawn when the Nile flood arrives, it is inferred that Sirius causes the Nile flood. Astrology is based on this sort of confusion. In Mesopotamia the sign for deity was a star. Cults of the sun and of the stars may have been growing up in this sort of way in Neolithic times. But really we do not know to what extent man had yet formulated any idea of divinity. It is difficult to distinguish ideas elaborated and diffused after the second revolution from those developed by the first.

VI / PRELUDE TO CIVILIZATION IN THE NEAR EAST

INTRODUCTION

Between 7000 B.C. and 6000 B.C. full-fledged agricultural settlements were established in southwest Asia, and these provided a solid foundation for the urban civilizations to follow. The most complete sequence of pre-urban development currently known is in the Kurdish foothills of northern Iraq and in adjacent parts of Turkey, Syria, and Iran. The best representation of the earliest Neolithic phase is in northeastern Iraq, at the site of Jarmo excavated after World War II by Robert J. Braidwood from the University of Chicago's Oriental Institute. This settlement, covering four or five acres, had an estimated population of 150 people, and, since the accumulated debris is over twenty-five feet thick, must have been occupied for at least a few centuries.

There is some confusion, however, regarding the date by which Jarmo was settled; it might possibly have been as early as about 6750 B.C.

Small rectangular houses with mud walls were erected in much the same fashion as Kurdish peasants build their homes today. The occupants of Jarmo cultivated wheat and barley as well as a variety of vegetables. They also raised goats, but it is not clear whether they domesticated sheep, pigs, or cattle as well. There are, however, enough remains of animals such as the gazelle to show that hunting was still of major importance; large numbers of pistachio nuts, acorns, and land-snail shells indicate other sources of wild foods.

The material culture of Jarmo is not especially impressive. Clay figurines of animals and human females were manufactured throughout the existence of the settlement. Pottery, on the other hand, was found only in the upper levels of the site. Some vessels carved out of soft stone were also uncovered. Domed ovens of clay may have been used for baking, and clay-plastered impressions in the house floors served as cooking pits. Flint sickles were used for harvesting, and the grain was pounded in stone mortars or ground on stone querns. One of the more interesting features at Jarmo was the use of obsidian, or volcanic glass, for making tools. Inasmuch as the closest deposits of this material are more than three hundred miles distant, the inhabitants of Jarmo must have been sufficiently well off to engage in trade for exotic raw materials.

A similar but somewhat later community characteristic of the Neolithic has been discovered at Hassuna and at a number of other sites in northern Iraq. The earliest level of settlement at Hassuna is anything but impressive: there are few signs of permanent structures, and implements made of quartzite or sandstone are extremely crude. In later levels, more elaborate housing appeared, and culminated in multiroomed dwellings built around an interior courtyard. Surplus grain was stored in bitumen-lined clay bins, and clay ovens were employed for baking. Some of the pottery is beautifully made, which suggests that people were spending more time working with new media such as clay or textiles than with stone. Female figurines known as "Mother Goddesses" again vaguely intimate some sort of fertility cult. The Mother Goddess complex later came to be widely distributed in the Mediterranean area, and ultimately was adopted even among Neolithic colonists and settlers in western Europe.

Before the end of the period represented by the occupations at Hassuna, a new Neolithic culture was taking root in the center of the Fertile Crescent. As this culture was first recognized at Tell Halaf, near the Syrian-Turkish border, it is called the Halafian. This cultural tradition is defined primarily on the basis of finely painted ceramics made in a variety of shapes and designs. Some authorities have expressed the opinion that the quality of this ware is so good as to have required full-time, professional craftsmen. Whether or not this is true, the pottery probably was fired in special kilns. During the Halafian period, many different kinds of amulets were carved of stone. Among these are stamp seals—button-like objects with geometric designs cut on one face so that they might be used to mark personal property by impressing the design into wet clay, much as one might seal a letter with wax. These are the prototypes of the stamp and cylinder seals found in Sumerian and later times.

The penetration of farmers into southern Iraq, the center of classic Mesopotamian civilizations, is marked by the appearance in that region of ceramics related to Halafian ware and to Samarran ware, a more or less contemporary ceramic tradition of the north. Such pottery has been found in the very oldest levels of the great mound, or *tell,* at Eridu, which was the first royal city of the Sumerians. Later, Eridu pottery was replaced by Ubaid ceramics, which came to be widely distributed in northern, as well as in southern, Iraq. The Ubaid pottery gives the impression of having been mass-produced, since it is notably inferior to some of the preceding pottery types. It is likely that the character of Ubaid pottery reflects nothing more than the attempt of farmers from the north to adjust to the south's alluvial floodplains. The profitable cultivation of the alluvium required some irrigation and the drainage of marshes. Once the Ubaid people gained a foothold, their settlement at Eridu became a town with an increasingly more substantial temple mound as its central feature. The Ubaid period, then, brings us to the threshold of Mesopotamian civilization at a time close to 4000 B. C.

Although the Ubaid tradition spread back up into northern Iraq and even as far as Syria and the Mediterranean, its true flowering was in the south. The scarcity there of stone and wood was overcome in part through the use of other raw materials. In architecture, considerable use was made of reeds and—as always—sun-baked mud, which was compressed into bricks for construction. Many implements, even axes and sickles, were made of fired clay. The earliest known sailing vessel is represented by a clay model from an Ubaidian grave at Eridu, and the use of plows and draught animals may have begun about this time. It was also during the Ubaid period that dates were first cultivated along the Tigris and Euphrates.

Other village-farming communities had been developing elsewhere in western Asia from the time of Hassuna. These have been described at Mersin and Byblos in Syro-Cilicia, Jericho in Palestine, and Sialk on the southwest Iranian plateau. The distinctions between different regions from the beginning presumably mean that the establishment of agriculture was more the result of new ideas spreading from one group to another than of migrations involving a single group of people.

A rather anomalous picture presents itself at Tell-es-Sultan, which is believed to be the site of biblical Jericho. According to radiocarbon determinations, the basal levels of Jericho are at least as old as Jarmo, but Jericho appears to have been a large town complete with stone walls, watchtowers, and a rock-cut defensive ditch. Underlying the earliest Neolithic levels, British archaeologists have discovered a pre-agricultural occupation site on which local hunters had erected a small structure that perhaps was a shrine. The relationship between the Jericho sequence and the Neolithic culture of Kurdistan can only be resolved by further archaeological work in both areas.

The following selection describes in the excavator's own words the discoveries at Jericho, beginning with the earliest occupation of local food-collectors and continuing up into the earliest food-producing levels (Proto-Neolithic A and B). These early Neolithic settlements have been described as the world's oldest towns.

◇   ◇   ◇

. . . Ancient Jericho is today represented by a mound about 10 acres in extent and about 70 feet high, on the outskirts of the oasis of modern Jericho. It owes its existence, as indeed does modern Jericho, to the magnificent perennial stream that wells up at its foot. The stream must draw its source from some underground reservoir fed by the rains on the uplands of Judaea, and it is vital to the life of Jericho. Rainfall in the Jordan Valley may be violent in winter, but in summer the great heat of this area, at Jericho c. 900 feet below sea level, dries everything up. Only in areas within reach of the waters of some permanent source such as that of the spring of Ain es Sultan at Jericho can the rich soil of the valley be made truly productive.

The mound of ancient Jericho is an emphatic witness to the importance of the spring. The whole of its 70 feet is the result of human occupation, covering a period of nearly seven thousand years. The spring today emerges at the eastern side of the tell, forcing its way out of the ground over a fairly wide area. The original source, perhaps a cave in the limestone, must lie buried beneath the debris of occupation, and has not been found. But it is clear from the evidence of the various areas excavated to bedrock that before there was any human occupation the surface of the rock sloped gently down from the west, from the ultimate foothills of the cliff-wall bounding the Jordan Valley, and that the spring must have broken out to the surface just at the point at which the hill slopes flatten off into the alluvial plain of the valley-bed.

Hunters may have visited the spring from the very earliest stages of the Paleolithic, as no doubt did the animals they hunted. One Paleolithic hand-axe was indeed found in a Neolithic level, but

From Kathleen Kenyon, *Archaeology in the Holy Land* (New York: Frederick A. Praeger, Inc., 1960), pp. 36-57. Copyright 1960 by Kathleen M. Kenyon. Reprinted by permission of Frederick A. Praeger, Inc.

there is no means of telling whether it was derived from the vicinity or from farther afield. The first definite evidence on the site concerns the Mesolithic period. On bedrock toward the north end of the tell excavations in 1958 revealed a curious structure. In this area the basic limestone was in its natural state covered by a layer of clay about a foot thick. Over most of the area excavated this clay had been removed by man, and the surface of the limestone exposed. But at the south end of the excavated area, a rectangle of the clay, 3.50 meters broad and more than 6.50 meters long, had been left, and had been enclosed by a substantial wall of stones, with wooden posts set in the wall at intervals. This structure was quite unlike any dwelling-house found on the site. Moreover, there were two other noteworthy features. Built into the wall were two large stone blocks, which had holes bored right through them, the total depth of the holes being about 2 feet 6 inches. They had obviously been intended to hold posts, and from their resemblance to flagpole sockets, one is tempted to suggest that they held totem poles, the primitive equivalent to flagpoles. Secondly, though the adjacent rock surface was covered with debris and rubbish, the surface of the clay platform had been kept scrupulously clean throughout the time it was in use. It is therefore possible that this curious structure was a sanctuary or some kind of holy place.

The interpretation of the structure is hypothetical, but its cultural setting is certain. From the associated debris were recovered a collection of objects which are certainly Natufian. Among the numerous microliths was a beautiful little lunate, and, most characteristic of all, there was a bone harpoon head. This is particularly important, since at Mount Carmel harpoon heads were found only in the Lower Natufian levels. Therefore it is certain that the first structure at Jericho was built by people allied to the first Mesolithic group in the Mount Carmel caves. Thus one can reasonably interpret it as a sanctuary established by Mesolithic hunters beside the source of the Jericho spring. Water sources have been held sacred by primitive people throughout the ages. Beautiful little votive objects have been found at the source of the Seine; many fine Romano-British objects have been found in the well of Coventina on the Roman Wall in Britain; and even today, in the Orient, rags will be attached to a tree beside a spring as a propitiation of the spirit of the spring.

Most fortunately for archaeologists, this structure was eventually burned down. The surrounding area was covered by charcoal from the beams that had been incorporated in it. This charcoal has provided a carbon 14 dating of 7800 B.C. ± 210. Even though, in our present state of knowledge, one must use carbon 14 dating with caution, for its reliability has still to stand up to the test of full experience, this dating has for the first time given us a relatively fixed point for the transitional stage in man's development into a civil-ized being.

The general background of the Mesolithic builders of this structure is certainly that of hunters and food-gatherers. But as we have seen, the inhabitants of the caves on Mount Carmel may have already been experimenting in agriculture, the prerequisite of any full settled occupation. The finds at Jericho show that these experiments laid the basis of success. Toward the center of the tell a highly significant discovery was made. Here were found a series of the Neolithic structures which are described below. But between them and bedrock was a deposit of 13 feet which produced no traces of any solid structure. A close study showed that this 13 feet was made up of innumerable floors bounded by slight humps which were all that remained of slight, hut-like structures. Therefore, for a very considerable length of time, people were living beside the spring of Jericho; living on the same spot, but still living in the sort of habitation suited to a nomadic, hunting type of life. Only after a length of time which, judging from the number of floors which went to the building up of this nucleus of the tell of 13 feet, was considerable, did they start to build solid structures.

Ultimately some genius led the way in building a solid house, and one can say that the first Palestinian architecture appears. These first houses have an obvious derivation from the primitive shelters, for they are round or curvilinear in plan, and the inward inclination of the surviving portions of the walls suggests that they had domed roofs. They are a translation into a solid medium of the impermanent huts of a nomadic population. Each has a projecting porch, in which is a stepped or sloping entrance leading down from a higher external level. The walls are constructed with hand-molded bricks, of the type known as plano-convex, with a flat base and a curved top, which often has a hog-backed silhouette. Sometimes wooden posts and wattling are incorporated in the walls.

The extent of the transitional, or Proto-Neolithic, settlement which produced the 13 feet of deposit without any substantial structure was apparently not large, for the deposit was found only in the one area. But the stage in which solid architecture was evolved was followed by a major expansion. The round houses have been found from end to end of the tell, covering an area which may be estimated at about 10 acres.[1]

The great interest of this development is that it derived directly from the first visits of the Natufian, Mesolithic hunters, which may be inferred from the Mesolithic structure. The same flint and bone industry, allied to the Lower Natufian of Mount Carmel, runs right through the transitional Proto-Neolithic stage to the large-scale settlement to which the designation Pre-Pottery Neolithic A has been given. Jericho has therefore provided evidence of the process for which archaeologists have long been looking, of the transition from man as a hunter to man as a member of a settled community.

After the settlement had expanded to its full size, it was surrounded by massive defenses, and assumed an urban character. The town wall was a solid, free-standing, stone affair 6 feet 6 inches wide. At the north and south ends as found it had been destroyed to its lower courses, but on the west side it was preserved to a height of 12 feet. At this point the excavated area coincided with the position of a great stone tower built against the inside of the wall, still surviving to a height of 30 feet. It is to be presumed that it was for the purpose of defense, and provision was made for manning the top by a passage entering from the eastern side, and leading to a steep flight of twenty-two steps climbing up to the top of the tower. The whole comprises an amazing bit of architecture.

The tower and defenses had a long history. Three main building phases in the tower and town wall can be traced. With the second town wall goes a rock-cut ditch, 27 feet wide and 9 feet deep. By the time [the third and final stage of the town wall] was built, the internal level had risen considerably, and on its inner side its lower part was not free-standing, but built against a fill. It still survives to a height of 25 feet. Subsequently a series of houses, of the usual curvilinear plan, was built against the tower and wall. The third in succession of these houses was burnt down, and the charcoal timbers lying on its floor provided material that gave a carbon 14 dating of 6850 B.C. $\pm$ 210. This date of course comes late in the history of the tower and defenses, which must date back to c. 7000 B.C.

The descendants of the Mesolithic hunters who had established their sanctuary by the spring at Jericho had therefore made remarkable progress. In the course of a period which carbon 14 evidence suggests is about a thousand years, they had made the full transition from a wandering to a settled existence in what must have

[1] This can only be an estimate, since the limits on the east side are uncertain, owing to the encroachment of the modern road.

been a community of considerable complexity, for the imposing defenses are evidence of an efficient communal organization. As we shall see, the earliest-known villages elsewhere are probably to be dated more than two thousand years later, and the pyramids of Egypt, the first great stone buildings of the Nile Valley, are four thousand years younger than the great tower of Jericho. The reasons for this development are obviously of great interest.

It may be inferred with a high degree of probability that this Pre-Pottery Neolithic A settlement of Jericho was based on a successful system of agriculture. Actual evidence of this is not yet available, as the samples which it is hoped will provide information about grain have not yet been examined. The inference can be made from the size of the settlement. A closely built-up area of about 10 acres might, by modern oriental standards, house a population of about two thousand people, and such a population could not have been supported on supplies of wild grain and wild animals obtainable within reach of the settlement. At a stage in the occupation of the site, which one may presume to be coincidental with the development of the nucleus-tell of 13 feet of deposit, the first experiments in agriculture, ascribed to their cave-dwelling predecessors on Mount Carmel and elsewhere, were developed by the Natufians at Jericho into the practice of regular food production. This produced sufficiently reliable supplies of food to enable them to settle permanently on the site and build the long succession of hut-like shelters. But the waters of the spring in its natural state would only have reached a limited area. Today, the widespread oasis is based on an elaborate system of irrigation. A further inference on the economy of Pre-Pottery Neolithic A Jericho can therefore be made. At a stage when the expanding population required a large area of fields, irrigation channels must have been constructed to carry the waters of the spring farther afield.

This inference has important implications. The successful practice of irrigation involves an elaborate control system. A system of main channels feeds subsidiary channels watering the fields when the necessary sluice-gate is closed. Therefore the channels must be planned, the length of time each farmer may take water by closing the sluice-gates must be established, and there must be some sanction to be used against those who contravene the regulations. The implications therefore are that there must be some central communal organization and the beginnings of a code of laws which the organization enforces. It has long been recognized that a major influence in the development of the villages of the valleys of the Nile and the

Tigris-Euphrates into towns and states was their dependence on irrigation, which both brought them great wealth and stimulated the evolution of urban characteristics.

The inference is that something of the same sort developed at Jericho. As regards evidence of the actual irrigation, it can never be more than inference, for all the area concerned is now covered by modern fields and irrigation channels. But the evidence that there was an efficient communal organization is to be seen in the great defensive system. The visual evidence that this provides links with the chain of reasoning based on the size of the settlement. The expansion of the settlement precedes the building of the defenses, and thus the need for irrigation had called into being the organization of which the defenses are evidence.

There were thus the greatest possible contrasts between the urban Natufian settlement at Jericho and the other settlements in which evidence of the stages developed from the Lower Natufian have been found. It looks as though there were two lines of development. One Lower Natufian group settled down at Jericho, and it is surely to be presumed that other groups established settlements in comparable positions. It is difficult to believe that Pre-Pottery Neolithic A Jericho developed in isolation; there must be comparable sites, but they have escaped observation, perhaps because they are not so large. But the cousins of the settled groups, living mainly in the hills, in areas less favorable for agriculture, continued in a Mesolithic way of life, still living as hunters and food-gatherers. The caves and shelters in which they lived have produced the implements which have been classified as Middle and Upper Natufian.

One of these sites, El Khiam near Bethlehem, is claimed to show a further transition. The flint industry which has for long been accepted as the classic Neolithic industry of Palestine is called the Tahunian. At El Khiam it is claimed that this develops out of the latest Natufian industry. This would therefore derive the Natufian groups from the descendants of the cousins of the settlers at Jericho. Not all authorities accept this derivation, and the alternative suggestion is that the Tahunian is superimposed on the Natufian. In this case we must bring the Tahunians in from outside, from a source not yet traced.

But though it is thus possible that the Tahunians are the descendants of the Natufians who long continued their nomadic way of life, they are certainly not the descendants of the settlers at Jericho. The Tahunians appear there, but only after a complete break. Wherever the Pre-Pottery Neolithic. A town of Jericho has been examined along the edge of the mount, the layers have suffered considerable erosion. In Trench I, on the west side of the tell, it is clear that the upper part of the town wall ultimately collapsed. The layers representing the successive houses built up against its inner side were eroded, as was the top of the tower, and the resultant debris filled up the ditch and piled up against the base of the town wall. By the time the debris had reached its angle of rest, the town wall was completely covered. In Site E, toward the north end of the site, a corresponding phase of erosion is represented by a stream bed, which cut down into the house levels in three successive phases before it finally silted up. Elsewhere the evidence is similar.

It is impossible to tell how long a period of time is covered by this phase of erosion. It may have taken place very quickly, or it may have covered a period of years or centuries. What is quite clear is that it marks the end of the occupation of the Pre-Pottery Neolithic A people. They may have been driven out, and their town destroyed, by their successors, or some disaster, such as an earthquake temporarily diverting the water supply and destroying the irrgation system, may have caused them to abandon the site.

These successors were an entirely different group, to which the name Pre-Pottery Neolithic B is given, and their flint industry is Tahunian. Almost all their other equipment also was different, for instance even the shape of the querns and of the grinding stones used with them. But most striking of all is the difference in architecture, which is described below, with large, many-roomed houses of rectilinear plan.

Historically, the most important point is that the newcomers arrived with this architecture already fully developed. Immediately above the layers of erosion appear houses of a remarkably stereotyped plan which lasts throughout the Pre-Pottery Neolithic B period at Jericho. This means that the newcomers had already behind them a sufficiently long period of settled occupation to develop an architecture, and even a detailed house plan, which was to serve their needs for a thousand years or more at Jericho. They were not, therefore, the immediate descendants of the Tahunians who lived at El Khiam, but of groups that had developed their own way of settled life. One might guess that their settlements were not far away, and that it was against them that the Pre-Pottery Neolithic A people had fortified their settlement, but here one enters the realms of hypothesis.

The houses of the Pre-Pottery Neolithic B phase are of very surprising architectural development. The rooms were mostly large, with wide doorways, sometimes flanked by timber posts. The plan of these rooms was rectangular, with slightly rounded corners, and the walls were straight and solid. The bricks of which the walls were constructed were made by hand (not in molds as is usual later), in shape rather like a flattened cigar, with the surface impressed with a herringbone pattern by pairs of prints of the brick-maker's thumbs, thus giving a keying for the mortar such as is provided by the hollow in modern bricks. Such bricks again are entirely different from those used by the A people. The floors were covered with a hard lime-plaster, often reddish or cream-colored, carried also up the walls, with its surface finished with a high burnish. The main rooms were flanked by small chambers, some of them apparently used for storage, and rain water was conserved in plastered vats built against the walls. The houses were built around courtyards, in which most of the cooking seems to have taken place, for the floors were found covered with thick charcoal layers.

The only utensils belonging to these people which have survived are stone bowls of various forms, the majority in a white limestone, finely worked and carefully finished. These vessels no doubt would have been supplemented by others of materials which have perished, probably of skin, and possibly of wood, though it is a curious fact that the tools found included very few suitable for heavy woodworking. The tools are mainly of flint or chert. The great majority are blades formed from flakes, which would have served as knives of all varieties and sizes. Some of the blades have been given fine serrated edges, and from the characteristic gloss that most of them bear it is clear that they were used as sickles to cut corn [grain] or grass; most are short sections which would have been set in a wooden haft; longer ones may have been provided with handles in the same manner as a knife. Other implements are borers and scrapers for use on skins. But, again in contrast to the A group, there are hardly any heavy tools which could have been used as axes, adzes or hoes, and it is difficult to see what implements were used to cut down trees; the use of some timber is attested by the sockets of posts in the walls, but it seems probable that wood was not extensively used. In addition to the cutting implements, there are innumerable hammer stones, pestles and polishing stones of all sizes.

Evidence of agriculture is provided by the sickles already mentioned, by the find of large numbers of querns and rubbers, and by the find of actual grain. The querns are of a standardized form, sub-rectangular, with a wide, flat rim round three sides, and the grinding hollow running out to the edge at one end. Cultivation of the ground was probably carried out by digging-sticks, pointed sticks weighted by stones, of which the evidence survives in the form of heavy stones pierced by a hole.

The implements found include arrowheads, some of them finely worked, but they do not form a high proportion of the total. Hunting therefore was an element in the economy of the inhabitants, but probably not an important element. Large numbers of animal bones found on the site, however, show that they were certainly meat-eaters. The only animal of which the skeletal remains suggest, in Professor Zeuner's opinion, evidence of domestication is the goat. However, in addition to this, there are great numbers of bones of pig, sheep, and cow. These can be described as potentially domesticable breeds, and not enough is yet known about the effect of domestication as revealed in the bones to decide whether they were still wild or were already herded. There are also great numbers of gazelle bones; these may have been hunted, but Professor Zeuner suggests that even they may have been herded, so as to keep them under control. The question of to what degree these Jerichoans were pastoralists, therefore, cannot be answered, but the scarcity of arrowheads in comparison with the great number of animal bones (and of other flint implements) suggests that they were.

The economy so far revealed is that typical of a Neolithic community, consisting of self-sufficient farmers, with some domesticated animals, but still obtaining some of their food supply by hunting. The self-sufficiency was not quite complete, for a few of the tools were made of obsidian, which was probably obtained from Anatolia. Some small lumps of turquoise matrix have also been found, which must have come from the Sinai Peninusla, and cowrie shells may have come from the Mediterranean. Such exceptions are quite usual in many Neolithic communities, for even in those early times a few luxury articles seem to have been obtained from distant sources.

The evidence of agriculture, the elaborate architecture, and the comparatively lavish equipment (even though it did not include pottery) show that these early inhabitants of Jericho formed a prosperous and highly organized community. There is also some evidence as to their spiritual and aesthetic development.

The principal concern of such a community would no doubt be the fertility of their fields and flocks. A number of little clay figurines of animals have been found, which were probably votive offerings to a supernatural power which was believed to control these things. More striking is a figurine of a woman, only some 2 inches high, an elegant little lady with flowing gown gathered at the waist, her arms akimbo and her hands beneath her breasts; unfortunately her head is missing. In attitude, the figure is typical of representations of the Mother Goddess common in much later cultures, and it is evidence that our early inhabitants already imagined a personified deity.

Another aspect of their approach to the deity is provided by a small shrine in a private house. The shrine was formed by blocking openings in the walls of one of the large rooms. In one of the walls of the small room so formed was a semicircular niche, at the base of which was set a rough stone to serve as a pedestal. In the debris of the house, not far away, was found a remarkable stone which exactly fitted the niche. It was of volcanic rock from the neighborhood of the Dead Sea. It had been elaborately flaked into a pillar of pointed oval section 1 foot 6 inches high. The unusualness of this object, and its probable association with the niche, strongly suggest that it had a cult significance, probably as a representation of the deity. It thus foreshadows the *mazzeboth* of the Canaanite religion of many centuries later, the stone pillars which are found on the sites of so many Semitic sanctuaries.

Another structure that might serve a religious purpose was a building with a central room 20 feet long and more than 12 feet wide, in the center of which was a carefully plastered and molded rectangular basin. At each end of the main room were annexes with rounded walls. The size, elaborateness, unusual plan, and central basin all suggest some ceremonial use.

The most remarkable finds of all at Jericho have implications both for the religion and the artistic capabilities of the Neolithic inhabitants. In 1952 a find was made which suggested that special reverence was paid to human skulls. This could be deduced from the skull of an elderly man which had been set carefully upright beneath the floor of one of the rooms, in the angle of two walls. The find suggested that his spirit was intended to remain in the house, and his wisdom to be preserved for its inhabitants. In 1953 a find was made which gave even greater evidence on the importance attached to skulls.

In the debris beneath the floor of one of the houses of the Pre-Pottery B stage there came to light a deposit of seven human skulls. Later two other similar skulls were found in another room of the same house. The lower part of these skulls had been covered with plaster, molded into the likeness of human features. Each head has a most individual character, and one cannot escape the impression that one is looking at real portraits. The eyes are inset in shells. In the case of six of the heads, the eyes are made of ordinary bivalve shells, with a vertical slit between two sections giving the appearance of the pupil. The seventh head has cowrie shells, and the horizontal opening of the shells gives him a distinctly sleepy expression. The molding of the features, mouth, nose, ears, and eyelids is fine and delicate, giving the impression that the people whose portraits we here see had small and well-fashioned features. The top of the skull is always left uncovered, though in one case the skull is painted with broad bands of dark paint, perhaps to represent a headdress. One curious fact is that in only one instance is the lower jaw present. In the rest, the chin is molded over the upper teeth, and the heads have therefore a somewhat squat appearance.

These heads give an amazing impression of the technical skill and artistic powers of their creators, totally unexpected at such an early date. They are not the oldest representations of the human form, nor even possibly the oldest portraits, for representations exist in Paleolithic and Mesolithic art. But they are far more lifelike than any earlier examples. Moreover, it can be claimed that they are the earliest human portraits directly ancestral to modern art. The art of the earlier epochs is divided by a gap of some thousands of years from subsequent developments, whereas from the Neolithic period onward civilization develops in an unbroken line, and the line of artistic achievement through the ancient Sumerian and Egyptian leads on to the Hellenic and so to the modern world.

The artistic importance of these heads is clear. But their cultural significance is more obscure. When found, the original seven were in a tumbled pile, obviously discarded when the house in which they had been treasured was ruined and succeeded by the next, beneath the floor of which they were buried. There was nothing in the part of the lower house that was uncovered to show whether they had been set in a shrine, or simply preserved in a dwelling house. But what was discovered was the source from which the skulls themselves must have been derived.

Beneath the floor of the lower house was found a large number of burials. Burial beneath the floors of the houses seems to have been the normal practice. What was exceptional was the very large number of individuals in the particular place, some forty or more within quite a small area. In some cases the skeletons were intact. In others the skull had been removed, leaving the lower jaw behind. In still others, the disturbance was much greater, but again hardly any skulls were found, and it looked as if a pile of partly decayed bodies had been searched through for the particular purpose of removing the skulls. The nine plastered heads did not account for by any means all the missing skulls, but the fact that the skulls had been carefully removed from the burials showed that they received special treatment, and almost certainly this is the source from which the nine skulls came.

Modern anthropological parallels would suggest that the heads preserved were either those of venerated ancestors or of enemies, kept as trophies. The only possible light on this is that such a mass of burials suggests some disaster. When the bodies were buried, there was at the same time built the first of the town walls belonging to the Pre-Pottery Neolithic B period; previous to this the town of the B people had apparently not been defended. This might suggest that a massacre by enemies had shown the necessity of providing defenses. The heads, on which too much loving care had been spent for it to be likely that they were enemies, might be those of important people killed in a massacre. But the evidence is slender, and is not borne out by any signs of injuries on the skeletons.

In 1958 another plastered skull was found far away at the north end of the tell. Moreover, as successive layers were excavated in all the different areas, skeletons were found from which the cranium had been removed. Though a corresponding number of plastered skulls was not found, it is clear that the removal of crania from burials was a regular practice; it is possible that they were removed to some central repository or shrine, which had not been located. It is therefore clear that the Jericho skulls are those of venerated ancestors and are not trophies.

From this practice of making portrait heads with an actual skull as a basis, there seems to have been a stylistic development. In the 1930–36 excavations, a very different kind of human representation was found. This consisted apparently of three almost life-sized figures of plaster, but of them only the head of one could be preserved. This head resembles the plastered skulls in the use of shells to represent the eyes, but in almost nothing else. The head in profile is a flat disk, and is thus a very stylized representation. There was some uncertainty as to whether these figures came from the Pre-Pottery Neolithic B levels or the succeeding Pottery Neolithic levels. Finds in 1958 make it probable that they belonged to the Pre-Pottery phase, for these seem to represent a further degree of stylization, and they came from the very top of the Pre-Pottery levels. They also may have been representations of complete, life-size figures, for many fragments were found. But the only one of which a substantial portion could be recovered extended only as far as the bust. The head (and numerous other fragments of heads) is now completely stylized, a spade-shaped disk without any attempt to render any features, and painted completely schematically. The shoulders and bust, however, are molded comparatively realistically. The three types of figures are most interesting evidence on the developments of primitive art. . . .

INTRODUCTION

The transition to agriculture in the Nile Valley appears to have taken place as the result of influences from southwestern Asia. The first farming communities by the Nile, as far as we can tell at the present time, were no earlier than the fifth millennium B. C., and while it is possible that certain plants and perhaps even cattle may have been independently domesticated in northern Africa, most of the basic crops and animals are of Asian type. On the other hand, when viewed in detail, the Nile cultures seem to reveal certain affinities with Negro Africa that suggest contributions from the south as well. Once agriculture was established in Egypt, however, the course of cultural development was largely a consequence of local initiative, and even before the Dynastic period (*c*. 3200 B. C.), one finds cultural patterns that are quite distinct from those of contemporary Asia and other parts of Africa. We know rather less about the Predynastic era than of later epochs, but clearly many of the roots of Pharaonic Egypt lie in this prehistoric "dawn of civilization."

Africa's Civilized Beginnings

Without prejudicing one's ideas by assuming there presently exist sides to join in the matter, it seems clear that there has been an understandable tendency to play down the African, and especially the

From Walter A. Fairservis, Jr., *The Ancient Kingdoms of the Nile*. Copyright © 1962 by Walter A. Fairservis, Jr. Reprinted by permission of Thomas Y. Crowell Company, The New American Library of World Literature, Inc., and the author.

early Egyptian, contributions [to civilization]. For one thing, except for the sudd regions of southern Sudan, there are no grassy slopes fringing the Nile Valley upon which wild goats and sheep frolicked and untamed barley and wheat flourished. To put it bluntly, there seem to have been no ancestors to these essentials of village life in Africa. Nevertheless it is not unlikely that there were experiments in early post-Ice Age Africa that contributed to the development of man's settled life. A well-known American anthropologist, G. P. Murdock, for example, has championed the theory that agriculture had another and independent origin in West Africa, not too long after its beginnings (c. 5000 B. C.) in western Asia (c. 8000 B. C.). The basis of his argument is primarily linguistic, since archaeological evidence is lacking for the present at least, and there is general absence of southwest Asian crops in the western Sudan even today.

> We should expect the particular people who first advanced from a hunting and gathering economy to an agricultural one to have multiplied in number and to have expanded geographically at the expense of their more backward neighbors, with the result that the group of languages which they spoke should have spread over an unusually wide expanse of territory. . . . Our criteria are fully satisfied . . . in the western Sudan by the far-flung Nigritic stock and particularly by its Mande subfamily, which centers on the upper Niger River. Not only do the speakers of Mande exhibit Negro agriculture in its fullest and most developed form, but their distribution demonstrates that they have spread in all directions at the expense of their immediate neighbors. . . .[1]

Murdock's list of plants indigenous to, and first domesticated in West Africa includes sorghum, Guinea yams, okra, calabash, watermelon, tamarind, cotton, and sesame along with varieties of cereal grains, peas, beans, and potatoes. This is an important list containing as it does a number of plants used all over the modern world. If Murdock's idea can be proved it places Africa in a far more important position in the ancient world than hitherto thought.

The trouble is that the evidence is still not of great strength. For instance, if cotton were first cultivated in West Africa several thousand years B. C. it would have to jump Egypt en route to India and then return somewhere around 550 B. C.—a not inconceivable event, but at least one that can be regarded as unlikely. Nevertheless, the theory stands on some logical facts, and, accordingly, we have to

[1] G. P. Murdock, *Africa: Its Peoples and Their Culture History* (New York: McGraw-Hill Book Company, 1959), pp. 66-67.

admit its possible contributions. For one thing, the processing of sorghum is not dissimilar to that of wheat or barley and it may well be that improvements on the western Asiatic grinding and baking techniques derived from Africa. The widespread use of sesame seed as a source of oil essential in the economy of the ancient world may have been a significant factor in the story of civilization. If so, West Africa's importance in ancient times can not be underrated.

Thus Egypt and Nubia may have been between two great farming developments by about 5000 B. C. But so far in archaeological studies of the prehistoric cultures, the Asian contribution appears strong and the West African very faint indeed.

In the Egyptian Fayum, settlements of hunters and fishers have been found. Here they also cultivated barley, wheat, and flax. Goats, sheep, pigs, and cattle were possibly domesticated, and the elaboration of arrowheads, groundstone axes, bone harpoons, and the possession of handmade pottery indicate that these people were advancing rapidly in their control of their environment. Bifacially flaked flint blades were inserted into a straight wooden handle to form an effective sickle. Perhaps of most importance were the subterranean silos lined with basketry for the storage of grain—the obvious preparation for that nonrainy day.

On the western edge of the Nile delta in Lower Egypt the site of Merimdeh is illustrative of a culture comparable in time and status to those of the Fayum (4500 B. C. and later). Here three phases of occupation indicate that construction of huts progressed from slight structures of reeds and poles, perhaps dabbed with mud, to strong, oval constructions surrounded by adobelike walls. Textiles were made—very likely from local plant fibers—and ivory, shell, and bone ornaments were probably used by men and women alike. Of great interest are the graves with their eastward-facing occupants flexed in what some like to call the "embryonic position." The fact that these graves were found among the houses of the villages indicates perhaps some belief in a spirit life after death where participation in the activities of the living could take place. It is suggestive of the historical Egyptian idea of an afterlife similar to the present life.

In Upper Egypt the site of El Tasa provides material evidence for a hunting-fishing group with limited grain agriculture and animal domestication. This culture was perhaps somewhat cruder than those of Lower Egypt (though perhaps of earlier date). They made pottery though, some of it quite handsomely decorated by pressing whitish paste into geometric incised designs on the surface of the sacklike vessels. The Tasians also buried their dead in the flexed or contracted position.

Whereas the people of these sites, insofar as we now know, were of the longheaded, rather slight Mediterranean racial stock, it is of interest that the people of the Badarian culture, which is more or less an elaboration of that of El Tasa and later in time, exhibit Negroid features. Was this because of African cultural contacts still not clearly defined? we might ask. There is no answer as yet except that the Badarian people appear to have been traders as well as hunters, fishers, and farmers. Copper ores like malachite may well have been imported from Nubia; ivory too may have had to come from the south as the supply of elephants and hippos diminished in the immediate Nile Valley. Wooden boomerangs may be of African derivation also. Of greatest importance, however, are the pottery models of boats which indicate an ability to maneuver up and down the Nile with more than a little dexterity. Excellent pottery, especially ripple-decorated ware, reveals a competence of craftsmanship undeniably derived from an exchange of ideas due to widening horizons. How wide those horizons were is tantalizingly suggested by the appearance of a similar pottery in the Sudan (Khartoum Mesolithic) and even west, across the Sahara, to the vicinity of Nigeria. The dating of these distant cultures, especially in the case of the Sahara, is completely uncertain, but associations of artifacts with the pottery indicate a time not too distant from that of the Badarian. Again Murdock's theory confronts us, for such evidence can indicate influences moving eastward as well as vice versa. For the moment at least we have no response!

In the Sudan, A. J. Arkell, leading archaeologist of the Sudan, has revealed two significant cultural entities both of which were apparently carried by Negroid peoples. The first of these has been labeled the "Khartoum Mesolithic culture." The type site is a low mound located northeast of the Khartoum central railway station. In ancient times this was the seat of a fishing settlement, though an ample number of swamp-living animals were also killed and eaten along with their aquatic companions the hippo and river turtle. The inhabitants had a stone tool repertory of various kinds of small-blade tools including backed blades, trapezoids, crescents, etc., usually found among Mesolithic bow-and-arrow hunters (or even Upper Paleolithic—i.e., Capsian). On the other hand they possessed grinding stones (probably for ocher), rubbing and polishing implements and a variety of pottery, some decorated with wavy lines not too unlike the later rippled ware found at Badari—which place the culture in a post-Mesolithic time context. Elaborations of bone harpoons, fishhooks, awls, and the like confirm this later affiliation. Direct indications of animal domestication and agriculture are nonexistent. However, grooved stones are evidence that they had nets or at least fishline, convincing proof of an advanced knowledge of fishing—the probable major basis of their economy. Woven impressions in pottery and in hard mud, the latter probably a remnant of wattle and daub house walls, are signs of an ability to plait and weave. As at Merimdeh, the dead were buried in the settlement in a contracted position but with no particular orientation and apparently without funerary equipment.

The presence of certain land snails (*Umicolaria flammata, Zootecus insularis*) revealed by their shells would seem to be clear indication that rainfall was heavier in the central Sudan during the time of the Khartoum Mesolithic than it is today. This appears to be confirmed by the skeletal remains of swamp-dwelling animals like the water rat and the Nile lechwe. There is also some botanical support. Such evidences of moisture conditions around 4000 B. C. and earlier are of interest since it does confirm an idea of a more prosperous land in late prehistoric times and the fact of its progressive desiccation with all that that implies in relation to the stresses and strains on nomadic and settled cultures.

A hunting-fishing culture with many of the tools and weapons of the Khartoum Mesolithic but with additions indicating an advancement in over-all technological progress was revealed by Arkell at the site of Esh Shaheinab. This ancient settlement is only some thirty miles north of Khartoum and is located on a gravel ridge, the remnant of an old river terrace, on the west bank of the Nile. The advances of the Esh-Shaheinab culture, now called the Khartoum Neolithic, are peculiar for a number of reasons. First there is the fact of the domestication of goats, the form being a kind of dwarf goat whose living descendant exists only in Algeria. Algeria, in fact, may have been the homeland of this goat and if so it again would indicate a west-to-east influx of ideas; though in this case the idea of domestication probably spread via North Africa to western Africa first. In any case, Arkell has put forth the interesting and certainly feasible idea that the advent of herds of goats with their inexorable consumption of all the vegetation in sight would have hastened the advance of desert conditions in those regions of Sahara that they frequented (e.g., Tibesti).

Another interesting feature of the Khartoum Neolithic (now

represented in the Sudan by at least two dozen sites distributed north and south of Khartoum in the Nile Valley, i.e., between Jebel Aulia and the Sixth Cataract) is the presence of certain kinds of pottery such as incised-rim black ware and black-topped red ware, both of which are familiar to archaeologists working among the cultures of Badarian and predynastic Egypt, but which may be earlier in the Sudan and thus illustrative of southern influences on the prehistoric cultures of Egypt. Though the Shaheinab culture belongs to a settled people the only evidences of settlement were the hearths and cooking holes. No reed shelters or adobe-walled huts were found and there were no graves anywhere to help to identify the inhabitants of the place, though the cultural similarities with the older Mesolithic culture suggest a basic Negro stock. Stone lip plugs also suggest an African current flowing steadily within the culture. Agriculture may or may not have been practiced—there simply is no evidence for it at the type site. However, Arkell places a point of tantalizing interest before us in view of Murdock's theories on West Africa as a place of origins. In one of the hearths he found:

> a carbonized fragment of the shell of the West African oil-palm Elaeis quineensis, identified at the Royal Botanic Gardens at Kew, whose Director calls attention to the possibility that the fruits, being important economically . . . may have been carried outside the natural habitat of the palm by human agency. It is known that the natural habitat of this palm is in West Africa. . . . No stress is, however, laid on this point; it is just mentioned as being of interest.[2]

Most remarkable of all the features of the Khartoum Neolithic are the close and important parallels with the Fayum Neolithic far to the north. Arkell lists these as:

> use of fireholes and very flimsy habitations
> disposal of the dead outside the settlement, by a method other than burial
> the domestication of animals
> the flaked and partly polished stone celt and stone gouge
> the burnishing of pottery, and
> the manufacture of beads from microline feldspar (amazon stone) [3]

When this evidence of things shared with the Neolithic of Lower Egypt is put alongside the evidence for the Fayum's undeniable sharing of many of its stone tool and weapon types with pre-

[2] A. J. Arkell, *Shaheinab* (London: Oxford University Press, 1953), p. 105.
[3] *Ibid.*, p. 104.

historic cultures in the Sahara, it would certainly seem as if both Lower Egypt and the central Sudan owe their Neolithic cultures in large part to areas to the west of the Nile Valley. As Arkell points out, even the bone harpoons of Shaheinab are more similar to those of the southern Sahara region (Wadi Azaouak) than to those of the Nile Valley.

This idea of a western homeland for the early cultures of Egypt and the Sudan is a very important one, but unfortunately evidence from the Sahara is only suggestive and not conclusive. To the layman reading thus far, the mysterious ways of archaeology may still seem mysterious, but as a science archaeology is as experimental as chemistry or physics. The proof for theories such as these can only come from more excavation, more study, and the testing of more theories. In this case the central Sahara and the Nile Valley are the obvious places of concentration. This serves to point up the desperate need to carry on field work in Nubia where the High Dam floods will bury the sites of prehistoric times. Even the date for the Khartoum Neolithic, based as it is on carbon 14 dating, is under fire. For the date of Esh Shaheinab is c. 3500-3000 B. C., which is much later than Fayum. A. Arkell disputes these dates in view of the clear parallels between the cultures: "But there are too many archaeological connexions between the Fayum Neolithic and the Khartoum Neolithic for it to seem reasonable to accept a difference of 800 years between the two cultures."[4]

The difficulties involved in assessing the validity of a carbon 14 sample have been shown in recent years to be multifold. It is not therefore unlikely that the Khartoum Neolithic is more nearly comparable in time of its Fayum counterpart.

But even with all the problems of dating and the scant evidence for origins, the outlines of a remarkable story are coming into full perception. The Old Stone Age hunting cultures of the Sahara were in contact with the early farmers who brought grain agriculture from western Asia. In the Fayum and at Merimdeh we have tangible traces of the hybrid cultures that resulted from this early mixture of Africa and Asia. Far to the south along the Nile Valley in stretches of Nubia and the central Sudan optimum hunting and fishing provided the basis for a settled existence almost as secure as that of farming. Pottery makes its appearance here and causes some archaeologists to feel that these early ceramics of the Khartoum Mesolithic were the earliest in the world. This early Sudanese settled culture looks to be almost purely African—the bulk of its tools and weapons

[4] *Ibid.*, p. 107.

derived from earlier and more westerly cultures and its pottery from local or more southerly cultures. The Khartoum Neolithic, with the Fayum, owes much to earlier cultures and much to the cultures around it. But what per cent is of Asia and what of Africa escapes us for the present. However, in view of the absence of good and ample evidence most archaeologists are inclined to consider the Nile Valley as the highway down which the advances of early Asiatic farming cultures found their way to Africa. C. B. M. McBurney, a profound student of the archaeology of northern Africa, summarizes the general consensus of opinion:

> Virtually nothing is known as yet of the Neolithic in that region [central Sahara] and in view of the evidence . . . the simplest working theory . . . is a general north-to-south process of diffusion and migration starting some time in the fifth millennium B.C. and ultimately originating in the Levantine coastal region.[5]

Whatever the origin of these cultures, progression from a simple to a more elaborate standard of living is manifest. Men were adapting to the environment not by moving about but by creating new means to control it. In the Nile Valley the simple settlements like Tasa and Badari were located on desert spurs protruding into the fertile alluvium. Though hunting was still a major pursuit, the richness of the annually flooded land became more and more apparent. Perhaps more and more individuals devoted themselves to the soil instead of hunting, the change-over occurring at first slowly but then more rapidly. Probably an influx of brown-skinned Mediterraneans from the north brought about the final conversion to a way of life that still endures, but which after 4000 B. C. was to create one of the splendors of the past—the civilization of ancient Egypt.

Some 2,670 years before the birth of Christ, Pharaoh Snefru, founder of Egypt's pyramid dynasty, the fourth, carried on a military campaign in Lower Nubia. His success was written in stone: "I brought back seven thousand prisoners, and two hundred thousand cattle, large and small."

Though these figures may be somewhat of an exaggeration, the event nonetheless is of great importance. It is obvious that for Nubia to furnish so large a booty there must have been some prosperity in that land. It is cattle especially that symbolize the kind of prosperity it was. Cattle require grass in some quantity and when grass-

---

[5] C. B. McBurney, *The Stone Age of Northern Africa* (Harmondsworth, England: Penguin Books, 1960), p. 244.

land is utilized for cultivation man has to supply fodder to maintain his cattle. Cattle, of course, have multifold uses, but one of the most important is as a draft animal. For these early agriculturists cattle supplied the energy resources that enabled them to bring all fertile land under cultivation and probably by means of cattle-motivated water wheels to irrigate normally arid lands. In any case it would appear that by the time of Egypt's Old Kingdom (*c.* 2680 B. C.,- 2258 B. C.) the narrow valley of Nubia and perhaps some of the watered places on the surrounding plateau were flourishing agricultural regions. In addition there were large numbers of pastoral nomads including the ancestors of the Beja peoples of the desert countries east of the Nile Valley. These nomads kept great numbers of cattle, sheep, and goats and moved from place to place with the seasons. A hardy lot living off the meat and dairy products of their herds, they were a considerably more difficult people to subdue than their more vulnerable and probably more pacific agricultural neighbors of the Nubian Nile Valley: or as it was known in those days, the land of Wawat.

In the previous chapter it was seen that in general Nubia and the Sudan kept cultural pace with Egypt up to about 3800 B.C. or until the time of the Badarian culture. But as Egypt's cultures continued their evolvement toward civilization those of the Sudan seem to have remained at a comparatively primitive stage. For one thing, agriculture appears to have been late in coming to the region. The American anthropologist Murdock feels that when agriculture did come it was of the west African type and that this was integrated with Egyptian-type agriculture in the Sudan. One fact seems certain and that is that there was little Egyptian influence on the Sudan for about eight hundred years. This was the more remarkable because those years cover the astounding developments of predynastic Egypt.

Early Predynastic Egypt (c. 4000-3500 B.C.)

Apparently deriving directly out of the older Badarian cultures, the first of the developmental steps of predynastic Egypt was the Amratian. This period witnessed the spread of grain and flax farming on a wide scale along the Nile Valley. Hunting was still continued as a supplement to the economy, however—almost as if there were a reluctance to give up ancestral ways of life or perhaps more because the early agriculture was still rife with uncertainties. However, the advances made in this period were considerable. Copper was sought for and pounded into needles and fishhooks. Fine flint was mined outside the grounds of the valley and even such luxury materials as gold and alabaster were brought from considerable distances. Slate was cut and smoothed into palettes on which malachite was ground into cosmetic powder. Some of these palettes were charmingly shaped into forms of fish and other animals. Most attractive of all perhaps were the carved ivories among which were combs topped with the forms of goats, giraffes, and birds. Animal drawing and painting was in great vogue in predynastic Egypt. On Amratian pottery scenes of elephants, sheep, giraffes, and hippopotami occur either scratched into the vessel surface or painted in cursive strokes with white paint. These drawings suggest relationships with the rock paintings and drawings found in the Sahara or even those of eastern Spain.

Two features of the Amratian are already symptomatic of certain culture features of the Egypt to come. One of these is the depiction of boats by the Amratian artists. These vessels were made of lashed bundles of papyrus and were propelled by oars: the sail, apparently, was unknown. No cataracts interrupt the Nile channel in Egypt and the development of boats made accessible the whole stretch of the river from Aswan to the Mediterranean. The increased use of the Nile as a highway anticipated the unity of cultural features which was to make Egypt unique in the ancient world.

A second feature of great importance is the obvious emphasis which the Amratians placed upon funerary custom. The cemeteries, which supply the greatest archaeological evidence for the period, attest the firm belief in an afterlife which is so profoundly Egyptian. In simple oval-shaped pits the body was interred in a contracted position surrounded by the objects of daily life. The harpoons, knives, sickles, maces, razors, arrows, beads, hooks, pins, and pottery which the deceased familiarly used in his everyday enterprises were placed with him in his grave, eloquent testimony to a simple but evolving way of life. Probably the objects were endowed with magical properties in order that they might continue their functions in the next world. There are even ivory or clay figurines representing servants and probably loved ones emphasizing by their presence the immortality of the wish that things might go on as they always did in spite of death.

Late Predynastic Egypt (c. 3500-2000 B.C.)

The Gerzean period, which follows the Amratian, demonstrates at once an elaboration on the earlier culture and the influx of new traditions, some of which were certainly Asian. Trade accelerates in this period not only along the river but overland: the latter probably because of increased use of the donkey, the true beast of burden. Not only was copper in great demand because of improved technology (including casting), but lead, silver, malachite, flint, ivory, lapis luzuli, and fine stone for vases were also required. The valley was by now largely under cultivation, though it appears that the marshy delta area was perhaps somewhat unevenly settled and was the seat for localized cultures. Towns grew out of some of the older villages and their mud buildings were well-made structures in which wood framing for doors and windows was relatively commonplace. These towns were the places where much of the nonfarming activity of the surrounding area was centered. Probably the specialized crafts such as those of metallurgy, ivory carving, shipbuilding, and the like, had their headquarters there. The support for such specialists derived from contributions made by the local farmers. At first it appears that these contributions were voluntary, but as society became more elaborate and the annual productivity of the land more certain and fruitful, controls tended to pass from the hands of individual farmers into those who held the political and thus the economic control of the towns. It appears obvious that as the individual farmers grew more dependent on the town specialists for their tools and luxuries, they also gave up a share of their independence in order to pay for them. The somber paradox of freedom-loving man caught in a materialistic world casts its shadow even in those remote days. Contributions turned into taxes, and what had been voluntary became enforced.

Whatever the reasons for the change, and admittedly we are speculating on some of these problems, it appears that the Gerzean was a time that witnessed both the expansion of trade and cultivation, and the acceleration of the centralization of Egyptian society.

It is notable that on the paint-decorated vases of the Gerzean period the scenes depict—besides animals, humans, and plants—boats of considerable size. These boats were usually marked by a standard. Set on an upright pole, which is fixed to one of the cabins, is an emblem such as a pair of horns, a harpoon, or an animal or bird effigy. Some of these emblems were used in historical times as representatives of various deities or in some cases as a kind of heraldic image of an administrative district or nome. Whereas it seems unlikely that predynastic Egypt was divided up into nomes, the ship standards may well indicate totems about which a body of traditions and beliefs had already gathered. That there were regions in which totemic elements were shared in common seems obvious from the historical evidence. In other words, it would appear that these early

Egyptians were aware of beliefs that they shared with neighboring villages but which were different from those held outside that portion of the valley or delta in which those villages were gathered. Each region had its town and this was the center not only for trade and news but apparently for the common worship of the local deities. There must have been in those days at least the beginnings of a priesthood in these towns, supported by the village farmers along with the other specialists. The extraordinary formal religion of ancient Egypt has its beginnings in this regionalization.

In later time, though state religion was generally acknowledged everywhere, the local deities and ceremonies were also recognized and maintained, even though features of this kind of dual worship were often contradictory. The multiplicity of deities so characteristic of ancient Egypt's pantheon owes its origin to this early "totemic" division, it would appear. Probably a certain family, clan, or even tribe had as its emblem a beast or bird whose unique powers were accredited to the social unit. Such designations as "the lion people," "the hippo people," and "the harpoon people" were probably used to identify these units. It appears as if at least some of these emblems were carried over from an early hunting tradition where, by sympathetic magic, animal qualities of strength, speed, and cunning were bestowed on the hunter. Perhaps it was during Gerzean times, when agriculture became the dominating pursuit of most of Egypt's people, that these emblems were given their more sedentary qualities familiar to history in such forms as Anubis, the jackal-headed god of embalming; Sekhmet, the warlike lioness goddess; or Thoth, ibis-headed god of wisdom.

The village rule in those ancient days was very probably in the hands of a chief whose post was hereditary, harking back to some totemic ancestor. Again, his chieftainship may have been a carry-over from hunting days. In predynastic times the chief very likely directed the communal activities, which included flood control and irrigation, village law, worship, and possibly the determination of the right time for planting and harvesting. It must be remembered that timing in the Nile Valley is a matter of considerable concern. The anticipation of the Nile flood and with it the measurement of the rise and fall of the river very early became the duties of a select group whose functions were closely entwined with religion. It is no surprise then, that in Pharaonic Egypt we find both the god-kings and priests involved in annual ceremonies in which river gauges play a major role. The early chiefs very speedily must have delegated such functions to others, which again anticipates the Pharaonic court with its host of officials, each of whom was responsible for some function.

It is unfortunate that we know so little about the Gerzean period. Much of the evidence may be buried irretrievably under the mud of the Nile delta. A large percentage of our information has to come from remains in the Nile Valley, that is, Upper Egypt. Nonetheless, we are aware that considerable activity was going on in the delta. The rich alluvium there must have attracted farmers from afar in spite of the marshes. Closer contact with Palestine and Sinai may have brought west Asian advances earlier than into the Valley itself. In any case some of the most important towns in Egypt's history were early located in the delta: Buto, Tanis, Bubastis, and Sais, among others. Significantly, the patron deity of the town of Behedit, Horus the falcon-god, who later became one of the chief gods of all Egypt, appears to have moved from his delta home to Hierakano-polis in Upper Egypt during the Gerzean period. Perhaps this move-ment is indicative of the true dawn of civilization.

INTRODUCTION

By at least the third millennium B.C., agricultural villages were established in Baluchistan, between the Indus River of West Pakistan and the Afghan frontier. A number of considerations again lead to the conclusion that western Asian sources provided the initial stimuli. Two factors are their relative proximity to western urban areas and their contemporaneity. Moreover, these settlements are too advanced in character to have arisen altogther independently, unless there are simpler antecedent cultures which have remained undiscovered. From these sites, which are really of Bronze Age rather than purely Neolithic type, have been recovered copperwork, painted and wheel-made pottery, and indications of fairly elaborate architecture—including what appear to be fortifications. Certain specific parallels to Iranian materials, especially ceramics, serve to confirm the existence of ties in that direction. These settlements are succeeded, in the Indus Valley proper, by the Harappan civilization, which, even at this early date, betrays some traces of modern Hindu cultural traits.

Most of what is known of this early civilization comes from the excavation of two sites, the city of Harappa, in the Punjab, and Mohenjo-daro, some four hundred miles away in Sind. The Harappan civilization appears to have been destroyed by Aryan invaders coming in from the north about 1500 B.C.

◇ ◇ ◇

. . . Before we describe the two principal cities which have been excavated, and the vast area they controlled, it is worthwhile to consider the most ancient sacred literature of India, the Vedic Hymns. There are about one thousand of them, and they are addressed to the greatest gods of the Hindu pantheon, extolling their deeds and entreating them to accept the sacrifice of their worshippers. The hymns are in Sanskrit, the literary language of ancient India, a branch of the Indo-European family of languages from which our own is descended. Parts of the *Rig Veda* may refer to the time before the Aryan invaders entered India, though this cannot be proved, but many appear to belong to a time of strife and conflict, when the invaders from the north were moving into the land to which they have given their name, a time when they called upon their greatest god, Indra, to help them in battle. Indra was "the ruler of the bright firmament." Like Zeus in Greek mythology he stands at the head of heaven as king of gods, and in Vedic poetry he is represented as performing wonderful deeds for the benefit of good men, while possessing at the same time the attributes of a war-god.

In some of the hymns Indra is *puramdaral* "fort-destroyer." To assist his protégé, Divadasa, he destroys "ninety forts." These are evidently walled cities of some sort; the word *pur* occurs, meaning "rampart" or "stronghold"; some are of stone (*asmamayi*), others probably of mud-brick (*ama*—"raw," "unbaked"). He also destroys one hundred "ancient castles" and "rends forts as age consumes a garment." [1]

Until recently it was assumed that these citadels were mythical, or, as Macdonnell and Keith suggested, "were merely places of refuge against attack, ramparts of hardened earth with pallisades and a ditch." But, just as in the case of the Homeric stories of ancient Greece, which used to be regarded as mere myths, the events described in the *Rig Veda* appear to have an historical basis.

In fact it can now be proved that when the Aryans entered India they had to encounter not mere untutored barbarians but a highly civilized people who had occupied the Indus Valley for at least a thousand years before the invasion.

The evidence for this has been obtained mainly from the excavation of two "lost cities." One is Harappa, already mentioned, a small town in the Montgomery district of the Punjab. The other is Mohenjo-daro, more than three hundred and fifty miles to the southwest. Mohenjo-daro is on the Indus; Harappa is on one of its

From *Lost Cities* by Leonard Cottrell. Copyright © 1957 by Leonard Cottrell. Reprinted by permission of Holt, Rinehart & Winston, Inc.

[1] For these allusions to the *Rig Veda* I am indebted to Sir Mortimer Wheeler's book *The Indus Age*.

tributaries, the Ravi. Between and beyond these two large cities, each three miles in circumference, archaeologists have identified sixty smaller settlements on the Indus Plain and more in the hills to the west, all of which have yielded evidence of a common civilization, though uniformity was greatest among the valley settlements. The total area covers more than one thousand miles from Rupar, at the foot of the Simla hills, to Sutkagendor, which lies close to the coast of the Arabian sea. This area is much greater than that of either ancient Egypt or Sumeria; in fact almost twice as large.

Anyone who has driven from Karachi across the Sind Desert will agree that this is not the most attractive area of the earth's surface. Where the Indus wanders slowly across the plain, it is bordered by a wide green band of vegetation, and here and there are areas which man has reclaimed from the desert by artificial irrigation; apart from these the eye has no rest from the monotonous, dun-colored desert, on which only the tough desert scrub and small bushy trees are able to survive. Throughout the long summer it grills under an unrelenting sun; on the windless days the heat-waves dance and eddy above the tamarisk trees; when there is a wind the blown dust stings the eyes. As the sun sucks from the earth the last vestiges of winter rain, a scum of salt rises to the surface, looking as one writer has expressed it, "like a satanic mockery of snow." Creaking bullock-carts move slowly along the dusty roads, linking the dusty villages from which. occasionally, the tall *stupa* of a Buddhist temple breaks the skyline. As in Babylonia, the modern traveler finds it hard to believe that such an apparently sterile land could have supported a numerous population.

As the traveler moves northward, following the great river, he sees, far away to his left, the hills of Baluchistan. Some three hundred miles from Karachi a tributary flows into the Indus. Following this for another hundred miles he reaches a point where another river, the Ravi, flows into it from the east, and fifty miles farther on, on the right bank, rises the extensive village of Harappa, overlaying part of a complex of mud-colored mounds. It was here, in 1921, that Sahni dug into the mounds and discovered evidences of a civilization which had existed for at least a thousand years before the Aryans entered the Indus Valley; we call it *Harappan*, after the site at which it was first found.

Harappa was a difficult and somewhat unrewarding site to excavate; difficult because the modern village occupies part of the mound, unrewarding because it had been largely wrecked by brick robbers who, in the nineteenth century, had extracted huge quantities of dried mud-bricks for use as ballast on the Lahore-Multan railway. Nevertheless, from the remains which survived, the excavators were able to establish that the city had a circuit of not less than three miles, and that its main features were a strongly-walled citadel on the west and a "lower city" to the east and southeast. The citadel, a rough parallelogram 460 yards long by 215 yards wide, was surrounded by a huge defensive wall of mud-brick, 45 feet wide, with an external revetment of baked brick 4 feet wide. Bastions projected at intervals to strengthen the defenses and there were ramps and terraces approached by gates, and supervised from guardrooms. The citadel stood on a brick platform, high above the plain, from which it was probably approached by flights of steps. The buildings which had stood within these defensive walls were too badly damaged to be identified.

When the archaeologists began to examine the mounds north of the citadel they were luckier. Here, close to the old river-bed (the river is now six miles away) three important groups of buildings were uncovered.

> Towards the south, close to the citadel, is a double range of barrack-like dwellings. Further north are remains of five rows of circular working-platforms; and beyond these is a double range of granaries on a revetted platform. The ensemble shows coordinated planning, and, although the methods of the excavators were not such as to yield stratigraphical evidence of the requisite intricacy, it may be supposed that the whole layout is of approximately one date.[2]

The two lines of barrack-like dwellings were incomplete, but sufficient survived to show that each dwelling consisted of two rooms, with floors partially paved with mud-brick, fronted and backed by narrow lanes, the whole being enclosed within a wall. "It is evident," writes Wheeler, "that the original scheme was both distinctive and uniform, and was in fact a piece of government planning. . . . It may here be added that on and about the site of these coolie-lines, but at higher levels, sixteen furnaces were found. . . . The precise function of these furnaces is doubtful, but a crucible used for melting bronze was found in the vicinity."

The seventeen circular brick "working-platforms" were evidently used for pounding grain. One had held a wooden mortar, and round the central hole where this had stood were fragments of straw or husk. Burned wheat and husked barley were found in another. It seems clear that on these platforms, arranged in regimented rows, all

[2] *Ibid.*

overlooked by the frowning walls of the citadel, laborers had wielded long wooden pestles, pounding the grain in mortars. A similar system is used in Kashmir today, but the sinister significance of the Harappa platforms was the evidence they provided of supervised and regimented labor.

About one hundred yards to the north of these platforms was a system of granaries, each 50 feet by 20 feet, also arranged symmetrically in rows, with a passage between them. The floor of each granary was supported clear of the ground by low walls, to allow the circulation of air. There were small projecting air vents, and the total floor space of all the granaries was over 9,000 square feet.

Somewhat later, archaeologists began to investigate the great mounds of Mohenjo-daro, nearly five hundred miles to the southwest in the Sind Province. Here there were few overlying modern buildings, save for a Buddhist *stupa* which rose above the highest mound.

When, after thousands of tons of earth had been removed, and the tangle of foundations, pavements and mighty walls stood naked to the sun, the least imaginative visitor was stirred to wonder. Throughout the world archaeologists recognized the discovery as a new landmark in prehistoric research; a new road had opened into the remote past of mankind. For here was a great city almost, if not as old, as the Pyramids or Ur of the Chaldees. The Nile, the Tigris, the Euphrates could no longer be regarded as the only begetters of the earliest riverine cultures. The Indus, now, could take her place beside them.

It soon became clear that Mohenjo-daro was a product of the same civilization which had created Harappa. Like that city, it consisted of two main elements, a powerful walled citadel to the east and a lower city to the west. The citadel was built on a platform of mud-bricks and mud, resting on an artificial mound. There were remains of defensive bastions at the southeast corner; two of them apparently guarded a postern gate, but at a later stage in the city's development this gate had been blocked and replaced by a platform, which had collapsed. Among its debris the excavators found "about a hundred baked-clay missiles, each approximately six ounces in weight."

Within the citadel the diggers came upon a huge bath or tank, 39 feet long, 23 feet broad, and sunk eight feet below the level of the courtyard, which was surrounded by a corridor separated from the courtyard by ranges of brick piers. Flights of steps led down into the bath, which had been rendered water-tight; the floor was of bricks set on edge with gypsum mortar between, and the walls were treated in the same way. The outlet from the bath led through "a high and corbel-arched drain which wound down the western side of the cita-del-mound." There were ranges of subsidiary rooms, one containing a well which supplied water for the bath, and there was a staircase leading up to the now-vanished upper story or flat roof.

Other suites of rooms, each including eight small bathrooms, were found north of the Great Bath, carefully and solidly built. Their well-made brick floors were drained by runnels communicating with a drain, and every room had a small brick staircase which presumably led to an upper story.

Even more remarkable than the Great Bath was a building lying to its west. It had first been detected by Mr. Ernest Mackay in the thirties; he had noted solid blocks of brickwork, each about five feet high, divided each from the other by narrow passages. Mackay thought that these might be the remains of a *hammam* or hot-air bath, but when the building was more or less completely cleared by Wheeler in 1950, its real purpose was revealed. It was the substruc-ture of an enormous granary, which originally had been 150 feet long and 75 feet wide, built, like the rest of the city, of mud-brick. When fully revealed some of the walls were found standing to a height of more than 20 feet. The outer walls of the massive platform were sloped, giving the building a grim, fortress-like appearance, and at the northern end was a brick platform, the walls of which were similarly sloped, save at one point where they were vertical, "evi-dently to facilitate the hauling up of bales deposited underneath."

The criss-cross arrangement of supporting walls was probably intended to assist air circulation, and there were vertical air-shafts let into the outer walls. The granary itself, of which only the platform remained, had been built of timber. In area it was approximately the same as the group of granaries found at Harappa.

Northeast of the Great Bath was another large building, substan-tially built, with a large open court and a number of small barrack-like rooms, some of which are carefully paved with bricks, and have staircases. It has been suggested that this was a "collegiate" building for priests, but this has yet to be proved. The buildings which lie underneath the Buddhist *stupa* and monastery cannot be touched at present; there are those who believe that there may be found the temple of the deity or deities worshiped by the Harappans. The arrangement of the citadels of Harappa and Mohenjo-daro recall the theocratic administrations of ancient Sumeria; at Ur for instance, the priests of the moon-god administered cloth factories, breweries, bak-eries and blacksmiths, on behalf of the god, and, of course, the state.

For the present this must remain pure speculation, since the written inscriptions found on Harappan sites cannot yet be deciphered.

For the time being, therefore, the lives of the ancient Harappans remain shadowy for us; all we can now know of them is derived from such of their buildings as have survived, and the objects found in them. But quite a lot can be learned. For instance, we know that they understood town-planning. The "lower city" of Mohenjo-daro was laid out in a criss-cross pattern of streets which were evidently planned from the start, unlike those of Ur, in Sumeria, which seem to wander inconsequentially. There is, however, something depressing and a little sinister in this huddle of lanes and streets, all built of mud-brick and, as far as can be ascertained, unornamented. Few windows opened on those streets, though there may have been grills for ventilation. Within, the chambers opened on to courtyards, and partitions were probably of matting, to assist in the circulation of air.

The most astonishing feature, which makes the Harappan cities almost unique in the pre-classical world of the ancient East, is the elaborate system of drainage and sanitation. Bathrooms are very much in evidence; there are latrines with waste-channels leading to cess-pits, which were evidently regularly cleared by municipal workmen.

> "The noteworthy and recurrent features," writes Wheeler, "are the insistence on water-supply, bathing and drainage, together with a substantial stairway to the upper floor. In some houses a built seat-latrine of Western type is included on the ground or first floor, with a sloping and sometimes stepped channel through the wall to a pottery receptacle or brick drain in the street outside." And of the general layout of the Lower City he says, "The main streets are about 30 feet wide, and major *insulae* or blocks are subdivided by lanes which are not infrequently dog-legged, as though (like the side-streets of Avignon, for example) to break the impact of the prevailing winds."

Besides private dwelling there were larger buildings which may have been industrial or commercial premises, and one, with conical pots sunk in the floor to take large jars, may have been a restaurant. Religious buildings have not been definitely identified, though the archaeologists discovered, in the Lower City, a complex of thick-walled buildings with a ceremonial approach leading to a central space which may have contained a sacred tree, or perhaps the statue of a deity. Near this building was found a piece of statuary representing a seated or possibly squatting man, bearded, with a shaven upper lip, and a fillet round his brow, which was subnaturally low. Like the other rare human figures found on Harappan sites, the face is prognathous and receding-chinned.

Up to date no examples of Harappan art have been found comparable in beauty and vitality to those of Babylonia or Egypt. A large number of terra-cotta and faience figurines have been found, mostly of animals. The human figure is rarely represented, and when it is, the work is often crude and carelessly executed, as if human beings mattered very little. Among the numerous statuettes of animals are the elephant, rhinoceros, bison, monkey, turtle, sheep, dog, pig, and various unidentified birds. These give some idea of the variety of wild animals which thronged the Indus Valley in these remote times, and suggest that four thousand years ago the area enjoyed a moister climate encouraging a marshy or jungle type of vegetation. A considerable number of small clay statuettes representing a female figure have been found; probably a goddess. Sometimes she is represented with a large, wide-spreading headdress and prominent breasts. Some of these figures have children at the breast; others have a pannier at each side, which, from the smoke stains sometimes found, were probably used for burning incense. She may have been the Harappan version of the "Mother Goddess" who was worshiped in many forms throughout the prehistoric world.

Some of the models are more skillfully made, such as tiny figurines made of faience (glazed paste) representing sheep, dogs, squirrels, and monkeys. Buttons, studs, finger-rings and bracelets have been found, made of this attractive green-blue substance. Gold beads have been found in a hoard of jewelry, probably the property of a goldsmith. Other stones used were carnelian and lapis-lazuli; steatite is used in quantity for such objects as beads and "pieces" for use on a games-board. Harappan parents made toys for their children, and there may have been professional toy-makers. There are model oxen with movable heads, model carts with terra-cotta wheels, figures of women kneading flour, whistles made in the shape of a hollow bird, pottery rattles with clay pellets inside.

The commerical aspect of Harappan life is emphasized by the numerous weights and measures which have been found on city-sites. The weights range from very large types, with lifting-rings attached, to small weights probably used by jewelers. They show consistent accuracy, and fall into a well-defined system. A decimal system was used for the higher weights; measures of length also followed a decimal system. A fragment of shell "rightly interpreted as part of a scale," was divided accurately into units of 0.264 ins., with "a mean error of 0.003 ins."

Irrigation was practiced, and remains of dams have been found to hold back the water of the river after the annual flooding. The Harappans grew, among other crops, wheat and barley, peas, melons, and on some of the seals there are representations of what may have been banana trees. They were also stock-farmers, raising sheep and cattle, pigs and goats. The camel appears to have been known, also the buffalo, the Indian bison, the bear, and spotted deer. They also kept domestic dogs and cats. At one Harappan site, Caanhu Daru, a brick was found over which a cat and a dog had run while the clay was still wet. The paw-marks were easily distinguishable, and says Mackay, "the deep impression of the pads and their spread indicated the speed of both animals." [3] The dog, as usual, was in pursuit.

Few noteworthy examples of Harappan art have been found; in general the better-finished statues, in alabaster, steatite and bronze, are stiff and formalized. Occasionally there are exceptions. One of the most interesting is a little figure of a dancing girl in bronze, found six feet below the surface-level of a house in Mohenjo-daro. It is nude; the head is provocatively thrown back, and the left arm is covered almost entirely from shoulder to wrist with bangles. She is of the aboriginal type, perhaps from Baluchistan, with a flat nose, curly hair and large eyes. The resemblance to Indian art of historical times is remarkable.

Other interesting similarities occur in the human or divine figures depicted on the tiny seals found on Harappan sites. One of these shows a figure seated on a low stool. The figure has three heads and is crowned by a tall headdress. The left arm is covered with bangles; on one side stands a buffalo, on the other a rhinoceros, and below the stool are two antelopes or goats. Sir John Marshall recognized in this figure the prototype of the Indian god Shiva, in his aspect as Pasupati, Lord of Beasts.

Occasionally one detects an affinity with the culture of Sumeria, with which the Harappans evidently had contact. For example, another seal has a representation of a figure with outstretched arms holding back lions. On another seal, which appears to have Sumerian affinities, a horned tiger is being attacked by a bull-man or "minotaur" reminiscent of the Sumerian Eabani created by the goddess Aruru to fight Gilgamesh.

No baked-clay tablets have been found, such as have revealed so

[3] Ernest Mackay, *The Indus Civilization* (London: Loval, Dickson, & Thompson, Ltd., 1953).

much of the civilizations of Babylonia, Assyria and the Hittite Empire. Some of the seals are inscribed in a pictographic form of writing which cannot be read, as it bears no resemblance to any known script, and no bilingual clue has yet been discovered. (I was informed that Mr. Michael Ventris, the brilliant young scholar who succeeded in deciphering the Minoan "Linear B" script of Crete—without a bilingual—was about to set about this equally difficult task. Unhappily, Ventris was tragically killed in a motor accident a few weeks before these lines were written.)

The problem of dating has still not been completely solved, but from objects of other known cultures found on Harappan sites archaeologists cautiously infer that the earliest date of the developed Harappan civilization (as represented by the cities) is not earlier than about 2500 B. C. However, both at Harappa and Mohenjo-daro there are still lower occupation levels which have not yet been examined. The rivers have risen considerably since these cities were built, and below a certain depth it is impossible to proceed without elaborate pumping-gear.

Did the Indus Valley civilization develop independently or was it in any way related to the earlier valley-cultures of Lower Mesopotamia? Informed opinion seems to be that while the Harappans, whose civilization apparently developed after that of Sumeria, may have received the *idea* from that area, they developed their own distinctive culture pattern independently of Mesopotamia. "Evidence for contact with the West before 2300 B. C.," writes Wheeler, "is not impressive." [4]

As for the closing dates, the Indus civilization appears to have continued well into the first half of the second millennium B. C., i.e., the time of the Aryan invasion of about 1500 B. C. The traditions recorded in the *Rig Veda* have taken on a new aspect since the discovery of Harappa and Mohenjo-daro. It now seems very possible that the "forts" and "castles" which the god Indra "rent as age consumed a garment" were the walled cities of the Harappans; not only Mohenjo-daro and Harappa itself but other fortified towns and villages of the same period which archaeologists have discovered along the river banks between and beyond the two principal cities. "Literary (or rather oral) tradition and archaeological inference have apparently more in common with each other than had previously been suspected."[5]

[4] *The Indus Age.*
[5] *Op. cit.*

The reasons for the decline of the Indus Valley civilization are not entirely clear. Some authorities suggest that climatic changes, a reduction in rainfall, may have altered the character of the land so that it could no longer support the abundance of plant and animal life on which the Harappan economic structure depended. This is a debatable point; if there were climatic changes, were they brought about through natural causes, or man-made ones; or both? The millions of kiln-dried bricks used in the construction of Mohenjo-daro, Harappa and other towns imply a large consumption of fuel for firing, and that certainly meant timber. Wood was also used extensively in Harappan buildings. Extensive felling of forests can alter a climate by reducing rainfall and encouraging soil erosion. It has happened in other parts of the world, and may have happened in the Indus Valley.

These at the moment can only be speculations, but it is certain, from an examination of the upper levels of Harappan cities, that in later years there was deterioration. The older, larger buildings were cut up into smaller rooms by partitions; the wide streets were encroached upon, lanes were choked with mean dwellings; clear evidence of political and economic decay. Yet the final blow which felled the tottering structure undoubtedly came from without. Dramatic evidence of armed attack was found at Mohenjo-daro and elsewhere.

In one room at Mohenjo-daro the excavators came upon the skeletons of thirteen women with a child, some wearing bracelets, beads and rings, in attitudes suggesting sudden death. One of the skulls had a sword-cut, and another showed signs of violence. Elsewhere in the city nine skeletons lay in strangely contorted attitudes in a shallow pit with two elephant tusks. It has been suggested that they are the remains of a family, possibly of ivory-workers, who in attempting to escape had been cut down by the attackers. The raiders may have looted the bodies but left the tusks, which would be of no value to them. One of the public "well-rooms" disclosed a scene of grim tragedy. "On the stairs were the skeletons of two persons, evidently lying where they died in a vain endeavor to use their last remaining strength to climb the stairs to the street. Remains of a third and fourth body were found close outside. There seems no doubt that these people were murdered." In other parts of the town skeletons had been buried in tumbled heaps, without the funerary equipment which would have accompanied them had they been formally buried. In other places the bodies had been left where they lay.

In the light of such evidence, which appears to date from about the middle of the second millennium—the traditional date of the Aryan invasion—there seems little doubt of the identity of the attackers. "Indra," as Sir Mortimer Wheeler comments, "stands accused."

The founders of Hindu civilization brought with them the cultural traditions of their Aryan homeland, but, even from the few examples of Harappan art which have been found to date, there seems no doubt that the elements of the civilization of the conquered were absorbed by the conquerors, though some were ignored, e.g., Harappan sanitary engineering. Eventually a time came when even the traditions of the ancient peoples were lost, their language forgotten, and their cities disappeared under mounds of earth and debris left by later occupiers. But from evidence accumulated by archaeologists during the past thirty years, more and more is being learned concerning this lost civilization. From a study of pottery styles, it has been possible to trace the beginnings of Harappan culture in the hill-villages of the upland valleys, where the remote ancestors of the city-builders of Harappa and Mohenjo-daro lived before descending to the plain. At one site, Jarmo, in the foot-hills of northern Iraq, radio-carbon datings have given 5000 b. c. or a little later as an approximate date.

Eventually, settlements grew up along the banks of the Indus and its tributaries, and gradually, an integrated society developed, apparently dominated by Mohenjo-daro and Harappa, twin capitals linked by the great rivers. In the absence of any written records, one can only speculate as to the type of society represented by those two cities, but they suggest a highly-disciplined state, drawing its tribute of grain on which the community depended, and storing it in the great granaries under the shadow of the citadels. The regimented rows of barrack-like buildings, the rows of platforms where the corn was ground under supervision, all suggest a powerful state organization, probably governed, as in Sumeria, by priests or priest-kings.

On the whole the picture is a grim one. While admiring the efficiency of Harappan planning and sanitary engineering, one's general impression of Harappan culture is unattractive. There is a drab, inhuman—almost subhuman—atmosphere about their cities; streets of plain, undecorated, mud-brick buildings, which, as Wheeler remarks, "however impressive quantitatively, and significant sociologically, are aesthetically miles of monotony."

One imagines those warrens of streets, baking under the fierce sun of the Punjab, as human ant-heaps, full of disciplined, energetic activity, supervised and controlled by a powerful, centralized state machine; a civilization in which there was little joy, much labor, and a strong emphasis on material things. Modern parallels are not difficult to find. Was this, perhaps "1984"—B. C.?

IX / THE ORIGINS OF CHINESE CIVILIZATION

INTRODUCTION

In China, as in India, the foundations of civilization are somewhat obscure, partly because the political disruption in China over the past quarter-century has impeded archaeological investigation. The earliest recognized farming populations, mostly in northern China around the Huangho, or Yellow, River, were relatively advanced and must either have developed through contact with the West or have evolved from a simpler—and as yet unknown—background. With the evidence available to us we have no means of determining which one, in fact, was the case. It is quite clear, however, that even at this stage a peculiarly Chinese way of life was already in the process of formation.

The Neolithic phase in northern China was followed by an urban Bronze Age, the Shang Dynasty, that was first recognized at An-yang in northern Honan Province, again in the Huangho basin. The Shang period may have begun as early as 2500 B. C., and includes sophisticated metallurgy, chariots, royal tombs, a system of writing, and intricate carving of jade, turquoise, and marble. The first written script appears on "oracle bones," pieces of bone or shell which were inscribed with questions addressed to the gods. This writing formed the basis for later Chinese script. Once more, certain elements, such as the chariots, bronze-working techniques, and royal tombs, are reminiscent of western Asia. Yet, even more than before, the culture as a whole is unmistakably Chinese. In view of the intensive caravan trade across Inner Asia in the first millennium B. C. and later (when adequate historical documentation is obtainable), it is not wholly inconceivable that there was sufficient contact between

East and West to promote cultural change in China and to account for some of the similarities.

◇   ◇   ◇

The origin of some of the noteworthy elements of the Shang culture may be traced directly to the Neolithic period. Most of the important Neolithic sites were located in the northern provinces, where there were in the prehistoric period at least four types of Neolithic culture. In the north of this region, a microlithic type known as the Gobi Culture flourished in the Gobi region, while in the south there were three sister cultures, Yang-shao, Lung-shan and Hsiao-t'un which had their origin in the Huangho basin. The development of these three latter Neolithic cultures simultaneously in the cradle of Chinese civilization had set the foundation upon which Shang culture was erected.

The Gobi culture produced some characteristic objects, notably a series of chipped stone tools fashioned in the microlithic tradition and a typical coarse brown pottery which is usually decorated with incised simple geometric designs. A number of the potsherds are comb-marked. Cultural remains of this type have been found mainly north of the Great Wall from Manchuria to Sinkiang. In several sites that have recently been investigated in the middle of the Huangho basin in eastern Shensi and Honan, microlithic implements, such as arrowheads and scrapers, have appeared in association with Shang remains. So it would not be at all farfetched to suggest that the Gobi culture did contribute something toward the rise of the Shang people.

The prehistoric culture in the Huangho basin presents, however, a different picture. The Neolithic remains in this region, from Shantung to Chinghai, appear to be basically uniform and the physical type of the population seems to have been similar to that of the modern northern Chinese. The people are known as the Proto-Chinese, a name first introduced by Davidson Black in 1925. In the late Neolithic period, this region was well populated. The Proto-Chinese were essentially agriculturalists who drew their sustenance mainly from what they could grow and supplemented their food supply by raising domestic animals, chiefly pigs and dogs. They lived in villages, which have been found to consist of underground pits used for dwelling and storage. In some cases the settlement was surrounded

Chêng Tê-k'un, *Archaeology in China*, Vol. II: *Shang China* (Cambridge, England: W. Heffer & Sons, 1960), pp. 239-49. Reprinted by permission of the author.

by a wall, more or less like a fortified city. All these features are common aspects of a Shang dwelling site.

The Proto-Chinese made a wide variety of stone implements fashioned by chipping, pecking, sawing, grinding and perforating. The common tools were axes, adzes, chisels and shouldered axes for cutting and digging; knives, semi-lunar and rectangular in shape and some with a handle, for cutting and harvesting; arrowheads, spearheads, sling-stones, *ko* dagger-axes for hunting and war; and perforated discs, rings and beads for spinning and ornaments. The raw materials for these included such fine stones as the *yü* jade. The entire lithic industry of the prehistoric period, including the materials, the techniques and the types of artifacts, was handed down to the Shang people, who improved upon it and soon succeeded in replacing it with an industry of metal. Most of the bronze tools and implements of the Shang period had their prototypes in the Neolithic period.

The origin of sericulture, one of the most notable features of Chinese civilization, may also be traced back to the prehistoric period. As early as 1926, an artificially cut cocoon of the *Bombyx mori* was unearthed by Li Chi from the Red Pottery site of Hsi-yin-ts'un in Shansi and this seems to indicate that the Proto-Chinese may have used silk in their textile industry. The craft became fully developed in the Shang dynasty. Silk fabrics have left their impressions on Shang bronzes and in the oracle script characters for silk and silkworm occur commonly. Besides, many spindle-whorls evidently used in connection with the industry have been found. Sericulture remained an exclusively Chinese cultural trait till recent historical times.

Some Proto-Chinese practiced scapulimancy. The cracks which gave the answers to inquiries were obtained by scorching a flat piece of animal bone. This was a simple outward manifestation of a complex system of religious beliefs, but in the hands of the Shang people it was elaborated and the animal scapula was soon replaced by the tortoise shell, which provided not only a standard size and shape but also a smooth surface with constant thickness. For almost every divination a record of the oracle was inscribed on the bone or shell itself, and it may be said that divination in this way assisted the invention and perfection of a written language thereby bringing China out of prehistory into the historical age.

It was probably owing to the diversity of the geographical environment that the Proto-Chinese came to produce three different types of pottery. The people in the loess highland in the west produced a Red Pottery which it sometimes painted; those who lived in the eastern flood plain made a Black Pottery which is usually highly polished; and those who lived further south in the Huai valley produced a Grey Pottery which is coarse and usually covered with beaten or stamped cord-marks. They are referred to in *Prehistoric China*[1] as Yang-shao, Lung-shan and the Hsiao-t'un respectively, because typical examples of these three types of Neolithic pottery were first reported from these three sites.[2] Archaeological evidence shows that in their respective areas these cultures appeared in their pure forms, but in the majority of the sites there is usually a mixture of these types. Of these three types of pottery found in various provinces the Grey ware of the Hsiao-t'un type was predominant. It seems that wherever it went the Hsiao-t'un culture absorbed and supplanted the other two.

In the later part of their development, some of the Proto-Chinese villages grew into towns and cities with industries of every description. The bronze age remains of the Shang people have always been found associated with the Grey Pottery, so it is stratigraphically clear that the Shang Chinese stemmed directly from the Grey Pottery culture. The Shang capitals at An-yang and Chêng-chou were built over Grey Pottery sites which were previously occupied by the Yang-shao Red Pottery and the Lung-shan Black Pottery peoples at separate intervals.

The region that covers the provinces of Honan, Hopei, Shansi and Shensi was known in Chinese history as Chung-yuan or the Central Plain. It is the border of the loess highland and the flood plain of Huangho. The course of events in history indicates that it was the center of Chinese life and that any rising power which had the advantage of controlling it would eventually become the ruler of the whole of China. The same situation may also be found in the prehistoric period. It is archaeologically clear that the expansion of the four Neolithic cultures, Gobi, Yang-shao, Lung-shan and Hsiao-t'un, tended to concentrate in this area, where their struggle for supremacy was most intense. As a result of their rivalry and coexistence, the archaeological sites in the area occur in a wide variety of combinations, some in successive stages while others are complicated mixtures.

The mixing of these cultures may also be noticed elsewhere in practically every province in China. To the north of the Great Wall many sites have been found with the mixing of the Gobi and the

[1] Volume I of *Archaeology in China,* by the same author [*ed.*].

[2] Hsiao-t'un is at An-yang [*ed.*].

Huangho cultures. They occur always in mixed forms, some dominated by the Yang-shao, others by the Lung-shan, a great majority by the Hsiao-t'un elements, many of which are associated with bronze objects and are definitely historical in date. The same situation has also been found in the Yangtse basin and in south China. Most of the southern sites present only the Huangho Neolithic elements in various stages of advance and in various degrees of combination with other cultures and are also mostly historical in date. In view of the fact that many of the Shang traits had their roots deeply embedded in the Neolithic past and that the Shang culture was surrounded and supported by a sea of Neolithic survivals, there seems to be no reason to doubt that the rise of the Shang culture was a logical outcome of the mixing of these Neolithic cultures. The process could only have happened in a region like the Central Plain where the cultural mixing took place.

The physical characteristics of the Shang Chinese are similar to those of the Proto-Chinese. There was, however, an evident increase of the brachycephalic elements in the composition of the Shang population as compared with the inhabitants of the prehistoric period. But this must not be taken as an indication of any fundamental change in the ethnical composition of the Shang population. The limited number of measurements and traits chosen for comparison scarcely justifies any basic conclusion of this kind. There may have been some mixing of physical types, but the majority of the Shang Chinese were essentially Mongoloid, just as the inhabitants of north China in the prehistoric period had been, and as the Chinese of historical times are. It is a well-known theory that the shovel-shaped upper incisors form a physical trait distinctly Mongolian in character. The almost universal presence of such a particular morphological feature among the Hou-chia-chuang skulls is sufficient to prove the racial affinity of the Shang Chinese to the Mongoloid race.

The Development of the Shang Culture

Since the fundamental stratum on which Shang culture was built was deeply rooted in the prehistoric past, a number of the Proto and Early Shang settlements were merely those of the Hsiao-t'un culture which existed side by side with the Gobi, the Yang-shao and the Lung-shan cultures. The beginning of the Shang may therefore safely be placed in the prehistoric period shortly after 2500 B. C. The stratigraphy revealed by various sites allows us to recognize at least five successive levels in the culture. They may be taken as five stages of development, namely, Proto, Early, Middle, Late and Post Shang.

The absolute dating of these five stages is still open for research. . . . Tung Tso-pin follows the traditional dating with some slight adjustments based on his study of the oracle records, believing that the dynastic Shang began in 1751 B. C., that the date for the moving of the capital to An-yang during the reign of P'an-kêng was 1384, and that the fall of the dynasty occurred in 1111. These figures give a total of 640 years for the duration of the dynasty. The fall of the capital at An-yang did not mean the disappearance of the Shang culture. In fact the Shang people continued to live under the Chou dynasty and kept their own identity for a long time afterwards. A period of about a century should be allowed for the contination of the Shang culture after the fall of its political power. It seems reasonable therefore to suggest that the Shang culture was in existence approximately from 2000-1000 B. C. The proposed dating of the five stages is roughly as follows:

1. Proto Shang (Neolithic) 2500-2100.
2. Early Shang (predynastic) 2100-1750.
3. Middle Shang (early dynastic) 1750-1400.
4. Late Shang (later dynastic) 1400-1100.
5. Post Shang (transitional Shang-Chou) 1100-1000 B. C.

The Shang excavations prove that in the early years of its development the Shang culture did not show any fundamental difference from the other Neolithic cultures of the Huangho basin, but in the Early and Middle Shang times new features began to appear and develop, reaching their climax in the Late Shang times. The progress was noticeable in practically every aspect of their life, covering not only the material culture and social organization but also their religious, intellectual and artistic activities. A large number of new cultural traits have been described in detail. . . . Ten of these may be picked out for special attention:

A. Material culture—
   1. Development in the ceramic industry;
   2. Development in carving;
   3. Development in bronze casting;
   4. Use of chariots;
   5. Development of architecture and chamber burials;
B. Social organization—
   6. Development of the feudal system;
   7. Development of ancestral worship;
C. Intellectual and artistic activities—

8. Development of the calendar;
9. Development of the animal style; and
10. Development of writing.

As far as our present knowledge goes all of these ten traits are features in which Shang culture made marked progress in advance of the four Neolithic cultures that flourished before.

There is no doubt that the greater part of the Shang ceramic wares was made in the Neolithic fashion. The Shang potter was aware of the existence of the Red and Painted Yang-shao and the Black Lung-shan wares. But while following their ways, the Shang industry experimented with some inventions of its own. Grey Stoneware which was sometimes covered with an extra coating of glaze appeared for the first time in Early Shang and continued in vogue throughout the rest of the dynasty. The White Pottery which was made of kaolin clay was first introduced in Middle Shang and its manufacture reached its height in the Late Shang period. There was a distinct change in both the style and the method of production of the more refined articles. We may safely conclude that the Shang potter was responsible for two major ceramic developments, the use of glaze and kaolin clay which set the industry on the right track and destined it to be one of the most famous Chinese contributions to art.

Carving had its beginning also in the Neolithic period when some of the basic techniques were already known. Most of the artifacts of the Proto and Early Shang periods, and a large number of those of the Middle Shang period are simple and clearly made in the Neolithic tradition; but in the Middle Shang period further development took place, the chief cause of which seems to have been the introduction of new techniques, notably the use of rotating apparatus. Many artifacts were then carved with a rotary wheel or drill. Carving reached its highest level in the Late Shang period, when bone, horn, shell, stone and jade carvings were abundantly produced. The techniques were followed and improved upon in the Chou period and the art continued to be a major means of expression throughout the Chinese history. Such is the craftsmanship of the Chinese that the carving of jade has almost become a symbol of Chinese culture.

Working in metal was a new discovery of the Shang Chinese. Articles made of almost pure metal, like copper, lead and gold have been found. Bronze articles made their first appearance, however, in the Early Shang levels. In the beginning the bronze technique was primitive and the finished products were crude and flimsy. Archaeological evidence shows that there was a gradual development not only in the use of the apparatus and the making of the alloy, but also in the shapes of the objects and in the decorative patterns. This industry too reached its height in the Late Shang period, when many complicated objects, some imitating the carved woodwork, were produced. The bronze art was an unique achievement of the Shang Chinese, since wine vessels in the shapes of the *chueh, chio, chia, ku* and *chih*, and cooking vessels such as the *ting, li* and *hsien* tripods are all unique forms. The decorative patterns of these bronzes are always unmistakably Shang in composition and in spirit. Many of these continued in use and were further developed in the Chou and later dynasties.

The same sequence of invention, use, and improvement was true of the evolution of military weapons. The development of the *ko* dagger-axe furnishes a good example, lasting more than a thousand years from the Shang period, through the long Chou dynasty, down to the third century B. C. The weapon finally merged with the spear-head and developed into the *chi* halberd, a characteristic weapon of the Han period. Li Chi traced the evolution of this particular fighting weapon and found that the *ko* of the Shang period was typologically the simplest, with a crude hafting technique, a blunt posterior part and no necking at all. The first development of the *hu* necking took place in the early Chou times and it gradually lengthened till it finally reached the standard type as recorded in the *K'ao kung chi*, which may be dated from the fourth to the third centuries B. C. Li is convinced that the morphological development of the *ko* throughout the Shang and Chou times indicates a systematic endeavor to improve the weapon through trial and error and a firm effort to achieve perfection. The weapon was thus invented by the Shang people and continuously developed by the Chou people without any interruption. The typological evolution of this weapon serves to link the Shang and the Chou culture together on a common foundation, which had never been so clear before the excavations.

The continuation of Shang industrial art into the Chou period may again be illustrated by reference to the bronzes and jades produced in the Post Shang period. It is well known that without adequate archaeological data it is most difficult to draw a line between the bronzes and jades of the Late Shang and the Early Chou periods. Nothing illustrates better the essential continuity of the arts of these two periods than this difficulty experienced by connoisseurs. In fact with the exception of a few inscriptions there are hardly any criteria to distinguish the bronzes and jades of the Shang period from those of the Chou period between 1100 and 1000 B. C. Most of the Shang artisans continued to supply the remaining Shang nobility and the new rulers with their wares. The style of art began to change gradually about 1000 B. C.

The fauna of the Yang-shao remains had consisted of pigs, dogs, and cattle; neither sheep nor horses were found. In the Lung-shan culture the list of animal bones had included those of pigs, dogs, sheep, oxen, and horses. In both cases deer were also found, but on the whole bones of wild animals had been rare in the Neolithic sites. This indicates a quiet life devoted entirely to agriculture and the keeping of a few domesticated animals. If there had been any game hunting it was limited to the hunting of a few deer. But the faunistic assemblage of the Shang culture, especially toward the later periods, is much more remarkable; the whole list of the mammalian collection being no fewer than twenty-nine in number. In the Middle Shang period we notice an increased use of the horse not only for riding but also for pulling chariots. The Late Shang chariot was drawn by either two or four horses in a team. The number gradually increased and in an early Chou tomb, twelve chariots were found together with seventy-two horses, which means an average of six in a team. It is well known that King Mu in the eleventh century B. C. used a chariot in his western expedition which enjoyed a team of eight selected horses. The Chinese chariot was invented by the Shang people and it continued to be improved upon in the Chou period. Toward the end of the Chou dynasty the power of a feudal state was counted by the number of war chariots which it possessed.

The development of architecture and of the structure of burial chambers also shows a steady improvement in the Shang period. In the beginning the people lived in underground dwellings in the Neolithic fashion, but in the Early Shang period we notice a gradual development until large ancestral temples and palaces were constructed according to prepared plans. Drainage systems and the careful preparation of the foundations with the *hang-t'u* technique[3] came into use.

The same may be said of the burial chamber. In the early days, most of the tombs were small and simple, but gradually the burial pit with a *yao-k'êng*[4] and tomb passages was introduced. It became larger and more and more elaborate until it reached its climax in the royal burials of Hou-chia-chuang and Wu-kuan-ts'un. These set the style for the burial of royal personages in later dynasties.

[3] Earth was stamped between wooden forms until very compact and then the forms were removed [*ed.*].

[4] A small sacrificial depository dug in the floor of a grave [*ed.*].

The Shang political and social organization was based primarily on the emergence of two social institutions, ancestral worship and the feudal system. We have no way of knowing how these began, but judging from the elaborate accounts in the oracle records there seems no doubt that they had long histories before the Late Shang period, and must have developed simultaneously with the expansion of the Shang kingdom. They exercised a strong influence on Chinese religious beliefs and social institutions in subsequent Chinese history. The organization of Shang society into two clearly defined strata, the warrior-nobility and the common people, was the beginning of the bifurcated society which has been the fundamental characteristic of the Chinese society ever since.

The rise and fall of the Conservative and the Progressive Schools[5] in the Late Shang period shows clearly that the keeping of the calendar was a living institution and it was being improved with the passage of time. The basic elements of the Shang calendar, including the naming and counting of the hours, days, weeks, months and years were all faithfully followed though with some improvements in later generations.

Although the use of animal shapes as decorations and ornaments in art may be noticed in the prehistoric times, the development of the Shang animal style from realistic to composite was unique. Although not very prominent in the earlier stages, in Late Shang this composite animal style exploded like a gigantic force to dominate the entire field of art. It is essentially symbolic, dominated by animal motifs, at the same time still retaining a number of geometric patterns. The achievement of this style may be attributed to the artist's freedom to take advantage of the experiences of others and to express himself according to his own will and imagination. The outcome was the creation and development of an artistic tradition, balanced in composition and highly individualistic in style, that not only led to further evolution in the Chou dynasty, as we shall see in the next volume, but also inspired many local developments in various regions surrounding the whole Pacific area. It was also in the same tradition that the Chinese *lung* dragon, *ch'i-lin* unicorn, and fantastic animal forms were created in the later centuries to suit the Chinese fancy.

Of all the cultural developments of the Shang dynasty none was more important than writing. The oldest form of Shang writing seems to have been the pictographical script which must have had its beginning in the very early Shang period if not in the Neolithic

[5] Two different groups of scholars and/or priests who apparently championed distinct forms of writing, time-keeping, divination, and ceremonies [*ed.*].

period. By the time of Middle and Late Shang it was already regarded as an archaic form of the script and was used mainly in personal and clan names which were found in the inscriptions of bronze objects. The development of the Shang kingdom made it necessary to improve on this early form of writing which, being pictographical in nature, was clumsy and complicated to write, or more exactly, to draw. The improvement was made by simplifying the form of each character. Throughout the entire Shang period some 3,000 characters were created for use and the script proved able to deal with the complicated demands made on it by the royal court and household. The study of the oracle script shows that the writing was already in service in the time of Wu-ting in the thirteenth century B. C., the forerunner of the form of Chinese script used throughout the centuries to the present day. It is interesting to note that whenever the characters in the Chinese script have seemed too complicated and cumbersome, they have been simplified in much the same way. Such a process is almost the standard method for improving the Chinese script and a new movement along the same lines is at the present time reshaping the Chinese writing with full government backing.

The excavations of Shang remains in China may be said to have brought to light the origin of the Chinese civilization. There is plenty of evidence to show that the Shang culture had already attained some of the most fundamental Chinese characteristics. It has been abundantly verified that the early historical Chinese civilization is essentially a north China creation of the native inhabitants. The region is continental, and by the time of the Neolithic period, a series of inidvidual cultures had been developed only to stimulate each other toward progress. Chinese culture was created by the activities of the Shang people in absorbing all the useful cultural elements within and beyond their kingdom. The Shang culture was the most prosperous as well as the most progressive one of its time, laying the foundation for an even more prosperous civilization in the following dynasties.

X / PEASANT FARMERS IN EUROPE

INTRODUCTION

Throughout the prehistoric period, which terminated only in Roman times, Europe north of the Alps was a marginal area outside the mainstream of Western civilization, and its cultural achievements were largely the result of contact with Mediterranean centers of innovation. Both agriculture and metallurgy, as well as many accompanying traits, can be traced to such sources.

By about 5000 B. C., peasant farmers from western Asia had begun to penetrate Greece and push northward to the Danube in the vicinity of Belgrade. Moving along the river and its tributaries, agriculturists practicing shifting cultivation occupied central Europe and reached the Rhineland no later than 4000 B. C. At the same time, other agricultural societies were being established along the islands and the northern shores of the Mediterranean. Ultimately these societies spread into Spain and France. Perhaps as early as 3000-2500 B. C., some cattle-herding Neolithic people reached England, and the Swiss lakes and southern Scandinavia were settled by farmers and herders about 2700-2600 B. C. It is likely that by 2000 B. C. the transition was complete except in the northernmost fringes of the continent. Local cultural diversity as seen in house types, ceramics, stone implements, mortuary patterns, and the like was very marked, and probably it would not be incorrect to assume that at least a part of the basis for historic differences between European peoples was formulated during this time.

The so-called Bronze Age of Europe began with the introduction of copper and bronze metallurgy about 1800 B. C., again through influences emanating from urban centers of the eastern Mediterranean. Along with copper and bronze were introduced other technological advancements such as wheeled vehicles and plows, but the major aspects of the Near Eastern Bronze Age—urbanization and writing—failed to appear. As a result, temperate Europe for the most part retained its Neolithic status other than in the partial substitution of metal for stone and some improvements in agricultural methods. The introduction of iron, beginning about 750-700 B. C., seems not to have been associated with drastic changes aside from the obvious advantage in toolmaking afforded by the use of a cheap and durable raw material, although there were some further developments in warfare and political organization (e.g., cavalry, the formation of feudal kingdoms).

Possibly the most notable accomplishment of prehistoric Europeans is to be seen in the monumental religious edifices and tombs constructed on the western side of the continent. Of all these, the great shrine of Stonehenge in southern England stands supreme. Here, late-Neolithic and Bronze Age peasants between 1900-1400 B. C. erected massive slabs of dressed stone weighing up to fifty tons each and carefully fitted curved capstones on top of them to form a continuous ring. Stones for the main circle were brought from a distance of eighteen miles, and some of the stones making up an interior circle and horseshoe were transported from an area in Wales about 135 miles distant even though they weighed up to four tons apiece. We do not know the exact function served by this monolithic structure, but there is considerable evidence to indicate that worship of the sun was involved.

◇   ◇   ◇

Stonehenge stands on Salisbury Plain, about eight miles north of Salisbury and a little more than two miles west of Amesbury. To the visitor who approaches the monument for the first time, particularly from the direction of Amesbury, the first glimpse is often keenly disappointing, for the stones, vast though they are, seem entirely dwarfed by the even vaster background of rolling Wiltshire downland. It is not until one approaches more closely, so that the stones are silhouetted against the sky, that the true size of the place becomes apparent, and begins to communicate to even the most casual and unfeeling visitor something of the awe and wonder with which it has for so many centuries been invested.

From *Stonehenge* by R. J. C. Atkinson (Hamish Hamilton, London). Copyright © 1956 by R. J. C. Atkinson. Reprinted by permission of Hamish Hamilton, Ltd., and the author.

The monument stands on a slight eminence of the chalk downs, but its position was evidently not chosen to command a particularly wide view. To the west the ground rises slightly; in all other directions it falls, though gently, the steepest slope being on the east, where the surface declines to the floor of a dry valley. In the immediate neighborhood of the stones the ground is almost level.

The details of the surrounding landscape are almost wholly man-made: the buildings of Larkhill Camp to the north; the sunlit hangars of Boscombe Down aerodrome on the eastern skyline; the massed birch trees of Fargo Plantation to the northwest; the long windbreak of conifers north-eastwards towards Durrington; and the two plantations of beeches, north of the Amesbury road, which conceal the cemetery of Bronze Age burials known as the Old and New King Barrows. Only to the south does something of the primitive landscape remain, where the skyline of Normanton Down is punctuated by the barrows of another cemetery. Happily, however, all the more obtrusively modern elements in the landscape lie at a moderate distance, so that even today the visitor, especially if he is fortunate enough to have the place to himself, can still sense something of that wild and treeless isolation which even the least sensitive observer must feel to be the proper setting for Stonehenge.

Of the nature of the original landscape of Stonehenge, at the time the monument was erected, we know nothing directly. We can be fairly sure, admittedly, that the actual conformation of the ground, the shapes of the skylines, the hills, and the valleys, have not changed appreciably. But of the vegetation, the grass, the bushes, the kinds and disposition of the trees, which clothe the bare bones of a landscape and give it its essential character, we have no evidence. The most one can say is that probably the ground was a good deal less bare than today, broken by at least occasional thickets of thorn, juniper, and gorse, and possibly by scattered but isolated trees. Even then, however, the effects of human occupation may have been apparent, though in a form less obtrusive than bricks and mortar. For nothing is more effective in clearing and keeping in check the natural vegetation than the continuous browsing of sheep and cattle; and it may well be that Stonehenge was originally set not in a thorny wilderness, but amid a carpet of short springy turf, even as it is today, created and maintained by the ceaseless wandering of prehistoric herdsmen and their flocks.

Of the stones themselves no words of mine can properly describe the subtle varieties of texture and color, or the uncountable effects of shifting light and shade. From a distance they have a silvery grey color in sunlight, which lightens to an almost metallic bluish-white against a background of storm clouds, an effect so notably recorded by Constable in his well-known water-color. When the ground is covered in snow in midwinter, with a dull leaden sky threatening further falls, they seem nearly black; and at sunset in midsummer their surfaces glow, as if from within, with a soft warm pinkish-orange light.

At a nearer view, each stone takes on its own individual pattern of color and texture. Some are almost white, like coarse marble, with the sparkling grain of white lump sugar, and so hard that even thirty-five centuries of weathering has not dimmed the irregular patches of polishing executed so laboriously by the original builders. Others are a dull matt grey, streaked and lined by close-set vertical cracks and fissures, like the grain of some vast stump of a petrified tree; and others again are soft, buff or even pink in color, and deeply eroded into hollows and overhangs in which a man may crouch, the compact curves of his limbs and the rounded thrust of shoulder and hip matching the time-smoothed protuberances of the stone around him. Here and there, the fine smooth grain of the stone is broken by small nodules of creamy or pinkish flint. And in places patches of a natural siliceous cement, like a thick weathered layer of amber lacquer, marks where the rock has split along a natural plane of cleavage.

On many of the surfaces, particularly on the lee side protected from the scouring force of wind and rain, there is a light growth of fluffy grey-green lichen, accented here and there by vivid patches of scaly yellow, which softens the contours of the stone, and half conceals, like a growth of fur, the scars left by those who have sought a little squalid immortality by the laborious incision of name or initials.

The huge mass of the stones, their upward taper, and the uncompromising four-squareness of the lintels which they support, together give an impression of forceful upward growth combined with an immense solidity and security. There is no top-heaviness, no feeling of impending ruin, even where an upright now leans from the perpendicular. Nor do the many stones which have fallen, and now lie half buried in the soil, give one any sense of cataclysmic destruction. Even their fall seems to have had a ponderous and purposeful deliberation.

To the inquiring observer the signs of man's handiwork are everywhere apparent: the squared and tapering forms of the stones; the severely functional shapes of the mortice and tenon joints on uprights and lintels; and the delicate rippled fluting of their tooled surfaces, like wave-patterns left on the sand by an ebbing tide. Yet these things, though they betray the hand of the mason, and alone allow us to confer upon Stonehenge the dignity of architecture, are nowhere obtrusive. Everywhere these specifically man-made forms are being etched and gnawed by remorseless time, so that the stone, having once yielded itself to the builders and suffered shaping to their purpose, now seems to be reasserting its own essential nature by the gradual obliteration of their handiwork. To me at least this stubborn yet imperceptible battle between the works of man and of nature, in which nature must inevitably triumph in the end, gives to Stonehenge a quality of immemorial antiquity and, at the same moment, of timeless permanence, that is lacking from all our other early prehistoric monuments, whose stones have only been chosen, but not shaped, by man.

All this, admittedly, is a private and personal vision, and some at least of my more austere colleagues would say that it has nothing whatever to do with the archaeology of Stonehenge. True enough, each man's vision of Stonehenge is particular, and none, perhaps, will much resemble my own. Yet even the archaeologist (perhaps, indeed, the archaeologist more than others) must look at his monuments not merely with a professional eye (an eye which too often is buried, ostrich-like, below the ground), but also with that wandering and passively receptive regard which, with practice, can penetrate beyond the surface to an inwardness which is none the less real or significant for being personal and, in part, at least, incommunicable. For who is to say that for the ultimate understanding of Stonehenge, not in terms of the categories of archaeological research, but as part of our human inheritance, and to that degree as part of ourselves, the aesthetic experience must play a lesser part than the precise and academic dissection of the evidence we recover from its soil?

XI / STONE RUINS OF SOUTHERN AFRICA

INTRODUCTION

We do not yet know all the details concerning the diffusion of agriculture and metallurgy into sub-Saharan Africa, but for most of the area it would appear that these are relatively late arrivals. Radiocarbon dating indicates that their appearance in central and southern Africa was during the centuries immediately preceding and following the birth of Christ. Technically speaking, we find here a direct transition from "Stone Age" to "Iron Age," since the first agriculturists were already using iron tools and weapons. The diffusion of iron metallurgy had caught up with the spread of cultivation and animal husbandry. Possibly, metal tools greatly aided agricultural progress by permitting more efficient exploitation of heavily forested country.

There is a regrettable tendency to play down the cultural accomplishments of African peoples, to the point where some of their achievements have been attributed to outsiders such as Greek and Phoenician traders, or even King Solomon. This has been particularly true with respect to the interpretation of various prehistoric building complexes of eastern and southern Africa, where one finds extensive irrigation terraces, fortifications, and settlements featuring stone construction. The most famous of these is Zimbabwe in Southern Rhodesia, although this is only one of about three hundred stone ruins in south central Africa. All sorts of theories have been devised to explain the origin of Zimbabwe, but it was almost certainly erected by local Africans during medieval times as the capital of a paramount chief or king.

◇   ◇   ◇

Great Zimbabwe is a group of stone ruins lying about seventeen miles southeast of Fort Victoria and a few miles from the main road which now links Salisbury, capital of Southern Rhodesia, with Johannesburg in South Africa. These ruins have their fame and reputation, among many ruins in Rhodesia, for their skillful putting together and their large conception, their tall girdling walls and towers, their rounded gateways, their evidence of power and unity and ordered settlement.

Two of its buildings stand out among the rest. Known as the "Acropolis," the first of these was a strong defensive structure on a hilltop. The second, known variously as "the temple" or "the elliptical building," rests on the plain beneath. All are made of local granite, of flat brick-like stones chopped skillfully from wide "leaves" of exfoliated rock which nature has slipped away from the parent hillsides. And the whole complex of buildings, whether in the valley or perched on the bouldered *kopje* overhead, has a dignity and strength of purpose in this lonely place that is irresistibly impressive.

At first glimpse these walls and terraced battlements will seem, as they seemed to stray explorers seventy and eighty years ago, the image of ancient structures in Mediterranean Europe. The impression of power and skill remains on being looked at closer, but the exotic image disappears. The more one ponders on these buildings the more they appear to have sprung from the native craftsmanship and ingenuity of peoples who worked here without any outside architectural influences to guide or help them. Everywhere these structures are marked with an originality which seems to owe nothing to the rest of the world.

It is not only that the walls abut on one another without bonding; this had been a common feature of Azanian[1] stonework, for example, and may be seen as far north as the walls of Jebel Uri in Darfur. It is rather that the fortress buildings seem to have grown naturally from the defensive convenience of huge boulders; and that the dwellings, where foundations remain, seem to have grown just as naturally from an attempt to build in stone what formerly had been built in mud and straw.

All around, after all, would have lain—as they still lie—great "leaves" of naturally split granite; it would have required little effort or invention, once the need and the incentive for strong and

[1] An East African stone-building complex [ed.].

conspicuous buidings were present, to break these into good stone "bricks," or to split away more "leaves" by building fires on the bare rock. Iron Age concentrations of power in this country, beginning here in the first millennium A. D. at much the same time as they began in the western Sudan, would infallibly provide both need and incentive—both the need for defense against rivals and the incentive for display of wealth and power. Here again there would occur the same general processes of power concentration—with the coming of metal technology and the social stresses, ambitions, and ideologies this would help to promote—as in other parts of the world.

With the passage of time, the simple piling of stone upon stone was elaborated into rounded gateways, timber-linteled doors, stepped recesses, closed passageways, platforms offering the slim silhouette of single-standing monoliths, and other features peculiar to Zimbabwe. And at last the girdling walls grew taller and stronger until they achieved the compelling power that may still be seen; the whole "elliptical building" being some three hundred feet long and two hundred and twenty feet broad, with girdling walls reaching to a height of thirty feet and a thickness of twenty feet.

These girdling walls surrounded the dwelling of the ruler of a powerful state. They were topped with a chevron decoration copied from coastal examples, seen by the traders and travelers and king's messengers who went back and forth across the plains and mountains to the ports of the Indian Ocean, or possibly invented on the spot. They guarded the mysteries of those who smelted gold and other minerals. Other walls nearby enclosed tall soapstone bird-gods and the temple homes of divine rulers whose powers of government had also grown with the years, but whose peoples had "chosen them to govern with equity." They towered above clay and stone settlements, clustered near, which became more numerous as the artisan and trading population multiplied. They imposed their reputation on coastal visitors whose strange reports would travel as far as maritime Europe, and suggest to learned gentlemen in libraries that the throne and seat of Prester John himself, legendary lord of inland Africa, was found at last.

The reports were embroidered; and yet, on reflection, by little enough. Though not the Prester John of a lost Christendom, the Monomotapa was a religious figure of no mean order. He was scarcely the lord of inland Africa; but he was certainly the lord of a state power, of a tribal-feudal organization, whose authority would have reached at its apogee across a land that was not much smaller than the Mali which his near-contemporary, Kankan Musa, had inherited. His court would not have glittered like the courts of the Holy Roman Empire, nor even like those of Plantagenet England; and his servants were illiterate. But it could have seemed neither poor nor unimposing to most of the men of his day, at least in Africa and Europe.

No Europeans reached it, so far as the record goes. None came here from the outside world but licensed traders and travelers from the coast, Africans and Arabs, who left no words of their own; and the manners of this inland civilization, its gods and customs, thoughts, beliefs and social growth, revolved only within their own native orbit. There was great development, but never a revolutionary break with tradition; no outside cultures intruded here and crossed their influence fruitfully with what they found. Yet the true greatness of achievement of these builders of the south may best be measured, no doubt, by this very isolation in which they dwelt.

INTRODUCTION

Recent archaeological work has shown that some American Indian agricultural systems have nearly as much antiquity as the earliest ones of the Old World. It is usually taken for granted that these developed independently, since the only feasible route of migration or diffusion from outside would have been via the Bering Strait—a region not at all suited to the transmission of agriculturally based economies. The sole alternative is to postulate impossibly long voyages across the Atlantic or Pacific, a thesis unacceptable to most archaeologists. Also, the very make-up of native American agricultural systems favors an independent origin; virtually all the cultivated plants (maize, beans, squash, potatoes, tobacco, and associated cultigens) were absent in the Old World, and none of the Old World domesticated animals was known in America before Columbus.

The earliest cultivation recognized thus far in the Western Hemisphere has been in the cultures of Peru, Mexico, and the southwestern United States, which were adapted to arid climatic conditions. Once established, plant domestication appears to have remained little more than an extension of food-collecting technology, and a long period of time elapsed before really intensive food-production promoted significant cultural changes leading to civilization. Why the implications of an agricultural economy were so slow in achieving realization is not readily apparent. Perhaps the general lack of domestic animals may have been a contributing factor.

◇　　◇　　◇

The change from food-collecting to a subsistence based upon plant cultivation was one of the great turning points in human prehistory. This is true of the New World as well as the Old, and there are indications in both hemispheres that this switch-over was not a rapid one, but that it was effected only over a period of experimentation. It is this era of experimental or incipient cultivation in the New World that I now wish to examine.

In the Americas it would appear that there may be at least four distinct and semi-independent traditions of incipient farming. Two of these are Nuclear American.[1] The northern one, the probable propagator of maize, was located in Middle America and in the adjacent deserts of northern Mexico and the southwestern United States; the southern one had its focus on the Peruvian coast. A third incipient-cultivation tradition centered somewhere in the tropical forests of the Amazon or Orinoco. Its existence is difficult to demonstrate archeologically, but such a tradition is needed to explain the domestication of manioc and other root crops. A fourth, and distinctly lesser, tradition rose in eastern North America in the Mississippi Valley system.

The earliest evidence for incipient cultivation in any of these traditions comes from northern Nuclear America. The region is the northeastern periphery of Middle America, in the semiarid hill country of Tamaulipas. Here, preserved plant remains were taken from the refuse deposits of dry caves. In the Infiernillo phase, dating from 7000 to 5000 B. C., there are traces of domesticated squash (*Cucurbita pepo*) and of possible domesticates of peppers, gourds, and small beans. The cultural context is that of North American desert food collectors. There are, in addition to flint implements, net bags of yucca and maguey cords and woven baskets of a rod-foundation type. In the succeeding Ocampo phase, from about 5000 to 3000 B. C., beans were definitely domesticates. After this, between 3000 and 2000 B. C., a primitive small-eared maize came into the sequence in the La Perra and Flacco phases. R. S. MacNeish, who excavated and studied the Tamaulipas caves, has estimated the composition of food refuse of the La Perra phase to be as follows: 76 per cent wild plants, 15 per cent animals, and 9 per cent cultigens. The La Perra and Flacco artifact inventories are not strikingly different from inventories of

Gordon Willey, "New World Prehistory." From *Science*, CXXXI, No. 3393 (January 8, 1960), 78-80. Copyright © 1960 by the American Association for the Advancement of Science. Reprinted by permission of the American Association for the Advancement of Science.

[1] That is, within the zone where later indigenous civilizations developed [*ed.*].

the earlier phases, although they demonstrate a somewhat greater variety of manufactures and an increased concern for seed foods. A few centuries later, at about 1500 B. C., an archeological complex which is representative of hilly settled village farming appears in the region. Thus, the Tamaulipas sequence offers a more or less unbroken story of the very slow transition from food collecting supplemented with incipient cultivation to the patterns of established cultivation.

Early and primitive maize is also found to the north of Tamaulipas, actually outside of Nuclear America, in New Mexico. At Bat Cave, corncobs from refuse of a Cochise-affiliated [Desert] culture date between 3500 and 2500 B. C. This is as early as the La Perra maize, or even earlier.

As yet, neither archeologists nor botanists have been able to determine the exact center of origin for domestication of maize in the New World, and it may be that this important event first took place in northern Middle America and in southwestern North America, where the intensive use of wild seeds in a food-collecting economy in a desert area provided a favorable setting. There remains, nevertheless, the very good possibility that a territory nearer the heart of Nuclear America and more centrally situated for the spread of maize in the hemisphere—an area such as southern Middle America— played this primary role in the cultivation of maize. The great difficulty is, of course, that the archeological record is so uneven, owing to the rarity of sites and environments where such things as plant remains are preserved in the earth. Such findings have not yet been reported in southern Middle America.

Coastal Peru, at the southern end of Nuclear America, provides a rainless climate and splendid conditions for preservation of organic materials in open archeological sites, and it is in Peru that we have glimpsed what appears to be a second tradition of incipient plant cultivation in Nuclear America. At Huaca Prieta, in a great hill of marine shells, sea-urchin spines, ash, and other debris, cultivated squash, peppers, gourds, cotton, and a local bean (Canavalia) were found, along with an abundance of wild root plants and fruits. The people who raised and gathered these crops and seafoods lived at Huaca Prieta at least 2000 years before the Christian Era. Whether there was, however indirectly, an exchange of domesticated plants between these early Peruvians and their contemporaries in Middle America is not certain. Such connections could have existed, or the beginnings of cultivation may have been truly independent of each other in these two areas of Nuclear America. Definite connections between early farmers of Middle America and of Peru appear, however, by 700 B. C. with the sudden presence of maize in Peru. This maize was not, like that at Bat Cave or in the La Perra culture of Tamaulipas, of an extremely primitive kind. It was brought, or it spread, to Peru as a relatively well-developed plant, and it serves as a link to Middle America. We may conclude that Nuclear America possessed, from this time forward, a single major horticultural tradition, but by this time we have also passed beyond the chronological limits of cultivation incipience.

An ancient tradition of plant cultivation in the South American tropical forest is based upon the presumption that a long period of experimentation was necessary for the domestication of such tropical root crops as bitter and sweet manioc (*Manihot utilissima, M. Api*) and the yam (*Ipomoea batatas*). It seems reasonably certain that these domesticates date back to before 1000 B. C. in lowland Venezuela. This is inferred from the presence of pottery griddles, of the sort used for cooking manioc cakes in later times, in the Saladero phase at the Orinoco Delta by this date. Also, the early archaeological phase of Momíl I, in Caribbean Colombia, has the pottery manioc griddle. The dating of Momíl I is debatable, but some of the ceramic traits suggest a date as early as 2000 B. C. Saladero and Momíl I are, however, outside the chronological and developmental range of incipient cultivation patterns. They appear to be village sites based upon the cultivation of root crops, and as such they are comparable to, although historically separate from, village farming based on maize. . . . For the present I bring these sites into the discussion because their existence implies centuries, or even millennia, of prior incipient root-crop cultivation in tropical northern South America.

A fourth tradition of incipient cultivation for the New World derives from the cultivation of local plants in the Mississippi Valley by as early as 1000 B. C. These plants include the sunflower, the goosefoot (*Chenopodium*), and the pumpkin (*Cucurbita pepo*). This domestication may have been in response to stimuli from Middle America, or it may have been an entirely independent development. This Eastern Woodland incipient-cultivation tradition was undoubtedly but a minor part of the food-collecting economy for a long time. Just how important it ever became, or how important the early diffusion of maize was to eastern United States cultures of the first millennium B. C., are crucial problems in the understanding of the area.

INTRODUCTION

When Pizarro and his small force of Spaniards arrived to conquer Peru early in the sixteenth century, they found flourishing there a remarkably advanced empire ruled by the Inca priest-kings. We have learned subsequently that the basis of this civilization, however much we may admire Inca political acumen, greatly antedates the emergence of the Inca state. As we saw in the previous chapter, these foundations can be traced back to at least 2500 B.C., when coastal Peruvians already possessed cultivated plants. Between 1200 and 500 B.C. in what archaeologists refer to as the "Formative" stage, the seeds of Andean civilization were sown. Within the centuries immediately following, achievements in technology, arts, crafts, and architecture reached their peak.

This Florescent, or Classic, period has been defined primarily through archaeological work in the arid coastal regions, where excellent preservation has stimulated more interest in excavation than have the damper highlands. Some of the textiles and ceramics manufactured during this time are scarcely exceeded in beauty and craftsmanship anywhere in the ancient or modern world. Metallurgical skills were expressed in work with gold, silver, and copper and included the techniques of casting, annealing, soldering, and gilding. Although most of the metalwork was for ornamentation, copper was used for some heavier, utilitarian objects. Massive stone architecture is seen in the construction of forts, temples, and truncated pyramids with stepped terraces that served as substructures for religious edifices. Private homes were built of sun-dried brick or stone. Religious ritual and ceremony were complex and involved special priesthoods and a pantheon of gods represented by anthropomorphic and zoomorphic deities. Worship of natural phenomena and ancestors appears to have been characteristic. Warfare was certainly an important aspect of life, in contrast to the Classic cultures of Middle America, and enemies were sacrificed or their heads taken as trophies. It is guessed that these practices had religious overtones.

Archaeologists have identified a major civilization on the north coast which they have termed "Mochica." Another well-defined one, on the south coast, is that of the Nazca people. The Mochica seem to have been more authoritarian, with something approaching a state religion, an emphasis on conquest, and rigid rank and class distinctions. From what we can tell, the Nazca had a more egalitarian society and greater religious freedom than the Mochica. It is perhaps because of this lack of authoritarian control that the public-works projects of the north are largely absent.

Since the Mochica realm is better documented, our remaining remarks are confined to that region. In addition to their flamboyant architectural and engineering feats, the Mochica produced effigy pottery and painted ware that graphically portray both everyday domestic life and affairs of state. We find, for example, that men wore ornate clothing which probably varied according to their status within the community. Prisoners, some of them possibly criminals, are depicted being stoned, mutilated by amputation, or flayed and exposed on the rack to await a slow death. Some of the ceramic art can even be taken to represent either portraits or caricatures of individual persons. The supposition that there were not only nobles and priests but perhaps also specialized classes of craftsmen, warriors, physicians, and slaves is corroborated by scenes painted on pottery. (Pornographic ceramics made by Mochica potters have not been ignored by either collectors or the late Dr. Kinsey.)

Economically, the Mochica depended mostly upon cultivation. Among the important crops were maize, beans, potatoes, sweet potatoes, peanuts, pumpkins, manioc, cotton, coca, pineapple, and papaya—most of which were to become vital additions to agricultural systems of the Old World when carried back by Europeans after conquest. The aridity of the north coast made it imperative that extensive canals and aqueducts be constructed to distribute water more evenly, and Mochica ingenuity in this sphere alone gives them a claim to fame. Fish probably provided a significant proportion of the diet, and meat was obtained mostly from domesticated llamas and guinea pigs. (Andeans were the only native Americans who engaged in the domestication of large animals, in this case the llama and alpaca.) Hunting is judged to have been essentially a sport for the upper classes, just as in Dynastic Egypt.

In spite of all these technological and artistic accomplishments, neither the Mochica nor their successors, as far as we know, had any form of writing or calendar. There are some suggestions, however, that they had at least a rudimentary understanding of mathematics and astronomy.

Another nuclear area of pre-Columbian civilizations was in the region running from central Mexico down into Guatemala and Honduras. In the valley of Mexico, the sequence began about 1400 B. C. with sedentary agricultural villages that by about 800 B. C. had a pyramidal temple mound as their central architectural feature, and culminated in this part of Middle America with the Aztecs and their capital city of Tenochtitlán. We know, however, that the Aztecs were by no means responsible for Mexican civilization, having come as nomadic barbarians into the valley of Mexico, where they ultimately rose to political supremacy in about the fourteenth century A. D. They were preceded, in the tenth or twelfth centuries, by the Toltecs, whose capital of Tollan lies in ruins just outside the modern town of Tula, Hidalgo. Approximately twenty-five miles from modern Mexico City is found the greatest urban center of altogether prehistoric date, Teotihuacán. This city, by some estimates, had fifty thousand or more inhabitants and was occupied as early as the third century A. D. It was destroyed between A. D. 900-1100 and was never rebuilt.

In southern Mexico, Guatemala, and Honduras, the Classic Mayas —at the peak of their cultural florescence—were contemporaries of the Teotihuacános. These two Indian groups, more than any other, are associated with three of the most notable achievements of the prehistoric New World: writing, mathematics, and astronomy. The Maya and their neighbors developed and used a type of hieroglyphic writing which has never been fully deciphered, and devised an intricate calendrical system based on sophisticated mathematics and amazingly accurate astronomical observations. Mayan mathematics included the concept of zero and positioning of numerals by units of twenty (that is, a vigesimal, rather than a decimal, system). The idea of a symbol for "nothingness" was arrived at at least once in the Old World, but it appears likely that the Mayas are to be credited with this highly important discovery on a quite independent basis. The Middle American solar calendar (there was also a religious calendar made up of lunar months) was better than that being used by the Spanish at the time of the Spanish Conquest, for our present Gregorian calendar was not adopted until A. D. 1582. Nor were the Mayas backward in art and architecture; we have learned a great deal about their arts through the excavation and study of their cities and ceremonial centers.

Below are described some of the Classic Middle American cultures —termed "Theocratic" because of the strong religious tenor all seem to have shared—with the intent of bringing into focus the life of these early peoples south of the border.

◇　　◇　　◇

Around 900 B. C. the egalitarian life of the simple farming community yields to increased complexity. The number and range of cultivated plants has increased: hunting is less important. Surpluses are larger and more dependable and need no longer be plowed back to meet needs of elementary subsistence; cultivation and its yields seem more assured. It was thus possible for groups of men to develop a lien on the disposal of that surplus, to employ it for ends which transcended subsistence. If it is true that man does not live by bread alone, he must first attend to gaining the daily bread that keeps him alive. Yet no human society restricts its purposes to the pursuit of the food quest; as soon as this basic need is met, it raises its sights and strives to transcend its earth-bound limitations.

This striving is evident in several ways in the tangible remains which the early Middle Americans left behind them. There is evidence of increased specialization and trade: pots are no longer made only for the home; they are also made for export. Shells, jade, turquoise are imported and exported. There are growing differences in burial offerings. A man is buried at Kaminaljuyú in a mound 20 feet high, and set to rest surrounded by 400 pots, jade, marble, greenstone vessels, jade-incrusted masks, pyrite mirrors, and ornaments of shell or bone. Another is interred without these marks of distinction. A social gulf yawns between the two members of the same society, a gulf which continues to separate them on their last journey and will continue to divide them in their after-life. In the valley of Mexico and elsewhere, we now find male figurines as well as female ones, many of them engaged in secular tasks; playing ball, holding dogs, or holding babies.

Reprinted from *Sons of the Shaking Earth* by Eric R. Wolf. Copyright © 1959 by the University of Chicago Press. Reprinted by permission of the University of Chicago Press.

Here we get our first glimpse of men set off from their fellows in appearance as well as in prerogatives. They are shown wearing masks over their faces, breastplates, cloaks, anklets, bracelets, hats; and only people so dressed are shown in the company of one or two female companions, or seated on a four-legged bench. Although these masked men are not yet stereotyped—details of dress and appearance differ from individual to individual—they are probably the first representatives of a social type which is to dominate Middle American society for close to two millennia. This man is the priest, set off from common humanity by dress, deportment, and skills, as well as by his vision of the universe and his dedication to the realization of this vision. In another way, 900 b. c. marks his emergence in Middle American society. To this date belong the first large-scale constructions built for a religious purpose—the prototypes of the burial mounds and temple platforms—which will provide the stage upon which these new specialists will enact their social role.

The development of differentiation between priest and common believer, hieratic intellectual and earth-bound peasant, is accompanied in many parts of Middle America by the spread of a distinctive art style, usually called Olmec by archaeologists. The origin of this style, the cultural characteristics of its carriers, and the depth and continuity of its influence are the subjects of much exciting speculation. The greatest Olmec site is at La Venta, a great ceremonial precinct erected on an island in the middle of a mangrove swamp in northern Tabasco, on the Gulf coast. But Olmec-style objects come from as far north as Tlatilco in the valley of Mexico, as far west as Guerrero, as far south as Costa Rica. Some of its works are dated at 900 b. c., but at the type site of La Venta the art style persisted until 400 b. c. Elsewhere, it may even have lasted longer. The features of this art style are highly distinctive, easily recognizable no matter where its manifestations may be found. Two of these features stand out strongly: a delight in carved jade and an obsession with the jaguar, an animal which these people represented in a multitude of forms. No other people has equaled the Olmec artists in their skillful use of jade, nor in the quantity of jade objects which they left in their sacred caches at La Venta or at Cerro de las Mesas. And no other Middle American artistic tradition has been so possessed by the feline form. The Olmec carved the jaguar into ceremonial axes and altars; the teeth, spots, and claws of the animal are depicted on pottery, ear plugs, and masks. Jaguar incisors are ground in jade. Human heads are marked with the tattoo mark of the jaguar; men are shown wearing jaguar skins; and human faces, centered upon jaguar-like mouths, acquire the features of the feline face.

We can only guess at the meaning which jade and the jaguar possessed for these eager idolaters. In Middle American religious tradition, the jaguar is associated with the god of rain and fertility, who was called Tlaloc among the Nahuatl-speakers, "He Who Makes the Plants Spring Up." One of Tlaloc's guises is the earth-god, who dwells in caves and mountains and possesses the "heart of the land." The jaguar is thus a symbol for the power that controls the heart of the land. But in the complex symbolic language of the area, caves and mountains also denote settlements and towns; and I incline to the view that the jaguar symbol is a symbol of domination not only over the sacred orifices of the earth but also over their human counterparts. Jaguar jaws are often found in Maya graves; thrones carved in the likeness of the jaguar are depicted in sculptured representations in the Maya area; headdresses portraying the jaguar adorn the Maya priests and rulers; and jaguar features mark the faces of gods as well as of men.

Jade was the most precious stone of Middle American lapidary art. Twenty-five centuries later, at the time of the Spanish Conquest of Middle America, when a noble died among the Mexica of the valley of Mexico or in Yucatán, a piece of jade was put into the man's mouth upon burial to represent his heart; a commoner received only a common green stone. The same use of jade is attested for Kaminaljuyú by A. D. 300. Again, we have a link between object used and nobility, uncommon status, domination, and rulership. These hints lead us to interpret the Olmec art style as the outward manifestation of a religious cult which also possessed strong political overtones. We get a view of new, rapacious deities; and this cult is linked to novel differences between men and men, associated with distinctions in function and in power. The Olmec art style spread so widely and exerted such lasting influence because it underlined the new lines of cleavage within the social order.

The change from food-gathering to the control of domesticated animals and plants involved a major change in technology, the harnessing to human ends of major new sources of energy. Was the growing complexity of the new ceremonial societies based on a similar shift in technology, or was it due rather to more efficient exploitation of potentialities already implicit in the older, corn-planter pattern? In the Old World, the shift from the egalitarian farming societies of the Neolithic to the class-structured, urban societies of the

Bronze Age involved both a heavy increase in productivity through the introduction and intensification of irrigation and the growth of new patterns of organization enforced by new ruling groups. We cannot be sure which of these phenomena came first. Some scholars believe that irrigation farming created the need for more efficient organization and coordination in the construction and maintenance of dams, dikes, and canals and in the supervision of workers who built and repaired these waterworks. Irrigation farming also produced the agricultural surpluses that fed both the laborers and the new organizers of production. Other scholars favor the opposite view and hold that the new patterns of organization came first and made the new productive enterprises possible.

Similar questions must occur to us when we ask ourselves how the new temple centers were provisioned. Some of them were probably mere cathedral towns, permanently inhabited only by a small group of religious caretakers but visited by the population of the surrounding countryside on certain holy days. Many of the centers of the tropical forest in the area of the Petén seem to have been of this type. Other centers, however, were clearly cities. One such city was the central Mexican metropolis of Teotihuacán.

Sanders has estimated the population of Teotihuacán at a minimum of 50,000 inhabitants, with the possibility that it may have been as high as 120,000. To support such a population on the basis of the two-field [rotation] system would require roughly between 150,000 and 400,000 acres, not counting an equal number of acres to sustain the producing population. . . .

If we cannot yet point with assurance to an ascertained body of facts which would show that the Theocratic period was ushered in by a set of technological changes, we can be certain that the organization of society had undergone a major change. The dominant figure of this new social order was the religious specialist, its center of power and ceremonial center. The center was a sacred precinct, divorced from the everyday routine tasks of the cultivator and set off from his huts. Within this precinct, the special apparatus was housed through which supernatural energy was concentrated, stored, and distributed to common men. This machinery was in the hands of uncommon men, priest-rulers, whose special training and esoteric knowledge allowed them to approach the deity and to transmit its will. These specialists wore the symbols of divinity, the mask of the jaguar or the feathers of the quetzal bird, and they spoke with the voice of gods. But they were not only devotees of the supernatural; they were also devotees of power, power over men. In them, society had developed a body not only of full-time religious practitioners, but also of specialists in organization, capable of exacting labor and tribute as well as worship from the mass of men. Such rule has been called theocratic; under it the power to rule and the power of religion are one. Ultimately, then, the social order is but an aspect of the universal order. If gods work to keep men in their place, and men labor to keep the gods in their heaven, the balance of society is properly maintained.

All early states were based on the combination of supernatural terror and secular power: the kings of China, Mesopotamia, Egypt, or Peru were sons of heaven or children of the sun, responsible in their exalted position to uphold the balance of the universe. They stood before their awed subjects in the splendor and terror of their godhood, but they also showered upon their subjects the benefits of peace and of a well-ordered social life, which was but an aspect of the well-ordered universe.

Painted murals and pottery of the Theocratic period show priests but seldom warriors. The leading figure of the society dominated by the ceremonial center is the full-time servant of the gods on whose mediation between supernatural and human beings the welfare of man depends. He is the steward of his gods on earth, their representative on earth. While he lives, he wears their symbols; when he is buried, these symbols are buried with him. In the name of the gods, he marshals labor to erect the gigantic pyramids, and in the name of the gods he exacts obedience from the men whom he controls.

Compared to the later Militarist period (A. D. 750-1519), there seems to have been little warfare, though it was not entirely absent. The only evidence of military power from Teotihuacán is a mural representing a warrior. He carries a spear, but the spear is decorated with plumes; his arrows are sheathed in protective balls. The glyphs of Monte Albán probably refer to towns defeated and conquered some time around the beginning of the Christian Era. Representations of men armed with clubs are fairly common in Olmec art. I am also inclined to think that the representations of heads hanging from the belts of Maya figures on stelae are not innocent decorative items but human trophy heads. Bound prisoners appear on Maya stelae, and human sacrifice seems to have been quite general, though the victims were mostly children and not adults, as in later times. The spear point found in the grave of a priest of Teotihuacán, moreover, may serve to remind us that coercion need not be directed only against foreign enemies; it can also be practiced against one's own people. Still, the Theocratic period seems to have differed from the later Militaristic both in the amount and in the kind of warfare practiced. The power of the priesthood was probably primarily ideological, though the spear, the club, and the arrow may never have been entirely absent from the scene.

The new specialists also possessed economic functions. Some of these functions were allied to their religious activities. Malinowski has shown us how the performance of magical rites can aid in the organization and timing of economic activities. The new priesthoods controlled the religious calendar which told people when to clear new land for planting, when to plant, when to weed, and when to harvest. Religious ceremonies were held to further the tasks of cultivation. The earliest representation of such a ceremony that has come down to us is probably the curious relief from a stone quarry in Jonacatepec, Morelos. The relief depicts three priests in Olmec style regalia; they hold spades in the air, while a fourth showers the land with his own seed from his erect penis. The priests of Tlaloc at Teotihuacán cast seed and water from their open hands; a personage wearing jaguar headgear is shown, in a Maya codex, planting corn with a planting stick. If irrigation was in use in Theocratic times, we may assume that the priesthood played a major role in its organization and in the distribution of the surpluses it produced. Where slash-and-burn cultivation was practiced, the priesthood probably played a part in allocating land to farmers and in regulating circulation upon the land, so that fertility could be maintained at high levels. Finally, it is possible that the temples served as deposits for seed from whch the next year's crop was raised.

The priests did not, however, serve only as administrators and organizers of agricultural effort. As servitors of their gods they also administered the many goods made as offerings to the deities. The temple centers became veritable storehouses of the gods, where costly produce accumulated in the service of the supernatural. Thus at Teotihuacán, we find shells imported from the two coasts, precious stones from Guerrero, rubber balls from the southern Gulf, mica from Oaxaca, feathers from the southern lands of the quetzal bird, and cotton from Morelos or from Veracruz. At Uaxactún, finds of obsidian, flint, grinding platforms, and mullers of granite and lava, jade, marble vases, shells from both oceans, and quetzal feathers bespeak continuous trade in the service of the gods. . . .

It is likely that the trade expeditions which traveled from one center to another were sponsored by the priests or were protected by them. Acosta Saignés has made the interesting suggestion that the professional traders of later Militarist Mesoamerica, the Pochteca, represent an old kinship group, with strong ties to the coastal regions of the Gulf. It may be that such intermediaries were the carriers of this trade in luxury goods from center to center. At the same time, there undoubtedly existed another kind of market, a popular market, in the shadow of the temples in which the peasantry around the ceremonial center brought their goods to the center of the gods either regularly, on a weekly basis, or more irregularly, in the course of pilgrimages. Permanent markets appear to have existed at Teotihuacán; in the Maya centers people probably came to weekly markets in the great squares. Still today, the Indian markets of Middle America are intimately linked with the centers of worship. The Indian comes to town to sell his goods; but he comes also to seek supernatural favors in the gold-incrusted dwelling place of his saints.

But the priests not only stored goods and sponsored trade. Like the ecclesiastical lords of medieval Europe, they probably employed craftsmen on their own behalf who produced on order to satisfy the requirements of cult and priestly display. One such group was perhaps the Amanteca, the kinship group of feather-workers, who later worked for the Mexica of Tenochtitlán. Their traditional association with Atzcapotzalco, where people from Teotihuacán sought refuge when that city was undergoing its final period of decline, makes it more than likely that they represent bearers of the older Teotihuacán tradition.

The center of this new order was always the temple precinct. In Middle America, as in other parts of the world, the temple precinct and its monuments were conceived as magically one with the supernatural world. Each precinct was oriented to the axes of the universe: north to south, as at La Venta and Monte Albán; or 17 degrees north of east, as at Teotihuacán, where the axis was in line with the point where the sun sets on the day of transit through its zenith, a day which also marked the beginning of the rainy season; or in relation to the solstices and the equinoxes, as at Uaxactún. The tiers of the temple pyramids were equated symbolically with the tiers of the universe, the pyramid itself with the mountain of the sky which the sun had to climb and descend to complete its daily circuit. Or a temple was but a magical replica of a world navel, as the great temple of Tenochtitlán, which was identified with the mythical Mountain of the Snakes where Hummingbird-on-the-Left leapt from the womb of his monster mother to slay the moon and the stars.

Within their replicas of the universal order, the priesthood labored in the daily rebuilding of order and consistency in the universe. In simple groups that must rely on hunting and gathering for their food supply and that lack permanent priesthoods, there are always individuals whose conceptual cast of mind leads them to grapple intellectually with the consistencies and inconsistencies of the world around them. The process remains individual and noncumulative, however, until there develops a body of specialists who see this intellectual labor as their duty and are rewarded by society for their efforts on its behalf. In Middle America, this effort at systematization, at making the universe routine and predictable, is evident in the abandonment of the traditional cult of the figurines or in its conventionalization; in the growing definition of a series of gods with specialized dominions; and in the development of priestly writing and of a calendar.

Figurines suddenly disappear in southern Mesoamerica over a wide area—in the Guatemalan highlands, in the Petén, in British Honduras. Elsewhere, to the north, figurines are sharply conventionalized and standardized by means of molds. The common folk are thus robbed of their ability to portray their deities or supernatural principles on their own. In contrast, the art of the tombs and temples acquires great rigor, severity, and austerity, in contrast to the more exuberant art of the folk.

Instead of the protean range of figures, a pantheon of gods emerges. The chief of these is He Who Makes the Plants Spring Up (Tlaloc), the god of rain and fertility. The Nahuatl-speakers called him Tlaloc; the Otomí, Muye; the Zapotec, Cocijo; the Mixtec, Dzaui; the Totonac, Tajín; the Maya of Yucatán, Chac; the Quiché of highland Guatemala, Tohil. In murals found at Teotihuacán he is depicted rising from the sea, with blessed rain dripping from his hands. His face is masked; the quetzal bird—symbol of rulership—spreads its wings above his head. Priests and servants stand on his left and right, sing his praises and pour out jewels and streams of seed. Men and butterflies disport themselves among the corn and flowers which grow along the shores of his watery paradise. Tlaloc's image appears as far south as Copán, in certain standardized associations with art forms symbolizing his several aspects. As jaguar, he represents the lord of the land who has claim to the earth, and its political and religious domination. As serpent, his undulating feathers represent the growing vegetation. The owl symbolizes his association with rainfall. In the esoteric sophisticated hieratic style which developed, these symbols could be combined as jaguar-serpents or serpent-butterflies to express in symbolic shorthand certain attributes of the deity.

Other gods, less important than Tlaloc, include a god of fire hunched under a bowl, a legacy of earlier times; a fat god who seems to have come from the Gulf coast and in later periods disappeared without a trace; a bat god, especially notable in the south among the Zapotec; and a masked personage who may be an ancestral form of Our Lord the Flayed One, in whose honor men were later—in the Militaristic period—sacrificed by flaying. If this interpretation is correct, human sacrifice probably existed at Teotihuacán. Self-torture in penance or in honor of the gods is also indicated by little incense burners shaped like candlestick holders, in which probably burned a mixture of copal gum and blood.

One of the great priestly accomplishments was the Mesoamerican calendar. All religions are interested in binding time. They gear the life-cycle of the individual to the recurrent rituals of society, and they synchronize this social time with the march of cosmic time. As the individual merges his life-span with that of society, he gains the security of knowing that his life will be lived in a rhythm which was there before he was born and will be there when he is gone. But even societies contemplate the infinite silence of cosmic space with fear and uncertainty. Calendar systems serve to bind this cosmic time, to domesticate it, as religion domesticates other aspects of the universe, and men derive comfort in visualizing the passage of cosmic time reduced to the mere sequence of cycles of social time. Different societies have possessed different cultural views of time. Some have pictured an original golden age desecrated by a single act, followed by a time of sin and guilt, which will end only when celestial trumpets announce a final judgment. Other societies have seen new cycles of time ever widening out in a continuous expansion of time. Middle American civilization was possessed by its own vision of time, in which the universe is not one but many, and in which each world, each universe, has its own allotted span of time that must inevitably end in catastrophe. When one universe collapses in flood or fire, another universe is born, though it too must come to a violent end.

The Middle American calendar system is the expression of this view of time. We do not know how it originated. The basic pattern may have been provided by a farmer's calendar, invented to measure agricultural time or the lapse of time between depletion and renewed fertility of land. Such a basic pattern may have been complicated by a magical concern associating numbers like two with a concept of cosmic duality; or four with the directions or with worlds created in the past; or five with evil caused by lack of measure and restraint. Such magical numerology may have been at the root of an original lunar count. Whatever the origins of the Middle American calendric system, it measures both recurrent social time and recurrent individual fate. It sets the time for celebrations and spiritual crises; it also allows the religious specialist to divine the future of men by interpreting the signs of days and their associated numbers.

The basic count (Nahuatl, *tonalpohualli;* Maya, *tzolkin*) combines 13 numbers and 20 signs like crocodile, wind, house, lizard, or snake into a count of 260 days. This calendar was clearly known to the priest of Teotihuacán and Monte Albán. Among the Nahuatl-speakers, Mixtec, Otomi, Huastec, Totonac, and Maya, this count was geared into a second count, a solar year of 365 days, composed of 18 months of 20 days each, plus 5 evil days at the year's end. The same combination of day number and day sign occurred in both counts every 52 years. Such a recurrent event the Mexica of the fourteenth and fifteenth centuries called *xiuhmolpilli,* a year knot or bundle. They felt that every 52 years the universe reached a cosmic crisis which threatened its survival, and men waited with bated breath to see the sun rise again in the continuation of a new cycle that might yet guarantee life to mankind for another 52 years.

In the southern part of the valley of Puebla (Tehuacán, Teotitlán del Camino) and in the Maya area, the priests carried the counts still further into a Venus year of 584 days. According to this count, the *tonalpohualli,* the solar year and the Venus year coincided at the end of every two 52-year cycles in another period of great supernatural crisis.

The lowland Maya appear to have taken these calendric calculations further than anyone else in Middle America. Only they seem to have developed a fixed starting point for their system, set at 3133 B. C. The date is clearly imaginary; the calendar itself probably originated around 500 B. C. Time was reckoned in ascending units (20 *kins* or days = 1 *uinal;* 18 *uinals* = 1 *tun;* 20 *tuns* = 1 *katun;* 20 *katuns* = 1 *baktun*). This reckoning was basic to the so-called Long Count practiced during most of the Theocratic period. Toward the end of the period, dates were abbreviated in a short count, which fixed the date accurately within a given lapse of time but which leaves us today wondering where the lapse of time belongs in relation to past or future lapses of time, just as a date written today as '58 could refer to 1958, 1858, or 1058.

Hand in hand with calendric calculations went the development of writing. Bars and dots for numerals were used by the Olmec, the inhabitants of Monte Albán, and the Maya-speakers of the Petén. The Teotihuacanos, Monte Albán, and the Theocratic Maya also made use of pictorial symbols to designate days and months. The oldest glyphs dealing with some sort of information which is not purely calendric appear on the Olmec Tuxtla statuette which bears a date of A. D. 162. The oldest phonetic elements in Middle American script seem to come from Monte Albán (Monte Albán II) where names of places were represented by additions of symbolic representations bearing phonetic value, in a manner later used by the Colhua Mexica. While we can read the calendric information on the Theocratic monuments, we are still largely unable to interpret the accompanying glyphs. Glyphs which may represent dates, and therefore the names of individual persons who were named after the day on which they were born, like "1 Reed," or "2 Rabbit," also appear on a number of objects associated with the Theocratic period. It is not impossible that such objects represent the first signs of clear-cut private property in luxury objects.

The priestly rulers also gave expression to their new power and the power of their gods in art. This art is often called "Classic." The term "Classic" is a stylistic term; it indicates that during this period there was not only a florescence of society but also a florescence in the forms of expression employed by this society. It is ultimately a term that refers to a culmination, a fruition of art forms; and indeed the Mesoamerican Theocratic period is such a period of culmination and fruition. Yet artistic style is inherently difficult to express in words, just as it is very difficult to evaluate. It is all too easy to let oneself be guided by Occidental notions of fulfilment in art, and to associate Classic florescence with sobriety and purity of line, while ascribing decadence to a love for riotous expression. Mesoamerican priestly art possessed at least two great artistic styles which we could call the Mexican and the Maya. The Mexican style came to fruition primarily in the central and southern highland; the Maya style dominated the rain-forest cities of the Petén. The Mexican style is geometric, monumental. The Maya style, on the other hand, loves riotous movements, luxuriant form, flamboyance. Both styles are equally Classic. Yet their difference denotes in all probability a wide divergence in basic values and feeling-tones.

The great contrast between these two styles is most apparent in public architecture. The Theocratic Mexican pyramids of Cuicuilco, Teotihuacán, Monte Albán, and Cholula emphasize horizontal lines. They are man-made mountains of superimposed tiers, rising slowly and ponderously toward the ceremonial hut at the summit, gigantic platforms for a celebration of the contact between man and the supernatural. The Theocratic Maya temple, on the other hand, strove for height. Its public façade was so designed as to give an impression of narrowness and height. The ascending platforms were narrow, the temple itself was small, and the roof of the temple was crowned with an exquisitely carved false front, the roof comb, architecturally an elaboration of the roof-crest on the Maya peasant hut.

Just as the two artistic traditions emphasized different values in their architecture, so they differed in the ways in which they decorated and adorned the walls of their buildings. Maya art is a kind of plastic calligraphy celebrating in undulant and rounded lines and a luxurious wealth of forms the ruling priests and their supernatural overlords. The Maya were marvelous draftsmen rather than marvelous sculptors. They "drew in stone"; their greatest achievement lay in the way in which they imparted almost three-dimensional qualities to the low relief that decorated their "artificial caves" and their calendric monuments. And at the center of their compositions, there always stood a human figure, usually a priest, or a priest with military attributes, and only exceptionally a god, shown in the great detail of his flamboyant feather headdress, belt, sandals, jewelry, and divine scepter. In sharp contrast, Mexican decorative art eschewed naturalistic and human representations in the decoration of public buildings. Its themes were supernatural; its mode of execution favored abstractions, carved three-dimensionally out of stone. Empty space always intervened between one set of carved abstractions and another, increasing the artistic impact through rhythm and repetition. . . .

The biggest and most influential center of Theocratic times appears to have been Teotihuacán, situated in a rather dry valley 25 miles northeast of Mexico City. Teotihuacán means "house of the gods." This designation can be interpreted in two ways. It may simply refer to a place of worship; or it may signify the place where the lords of the people woke from the dream of life and became gods. Sahagún, the Franciscan friar to whom we owe such a great deal of our knowledge of pre-Hispanic Middle America, tells an ancient tale according to which, "From Tamoanchan they traveled to offer sacrifices at the town called Teutihoacán, where they built two mountains in honor of the sun and the moon, and in this town those who were to reign over the others were elected, for which it was called Teutiocan, which means Veitoacan, or the place where they made signs. There the most important lords were buried."

The city may well have been the largest settlement in Middle America. It grew from a size of 700 acres before A. D. 350 to 2,000 acres in another three centuries. On aerial photographs, the densely settled area within the city limits shows up clearly in contrast with the open fields of the surrounding countryside. The oldest dated remains at the site are assigned to the time of Christ, though the Pyramid of the Moon—the second largest pyramid of the site, measuring 495 by 405 feet at the base and 140 feet in height—is probably older. The big temples were built or rebuilt several times between the time of Christ and A. D. 250. Teotihuacán was finally destroyed and abandoned around A. D. 800. The fury of destruction is recorded for posterity in a thick gray layer of ash which shows that the city was put to the torch.

The settlement pattern is laid out along a main axis, 60 yards wide, formed by the Avenue of the Dead. It takes its origin at the Pyramid of the Moon, runs past the Pyramid of the Sun and the temple precinct of the Feathered Serpent; most of the civic and religious buildings are located along it, as are the wealthy residential buildings. Small streets lead off the avenue into the popular quarters of the city where people lived in crowded quarters separated by small courtyards and alleyways. Each quarter seems to have had its own religious center, suggesting that the pattern of main center, satellite centers, and dependent communities is very ancient in Middle America. Large open squares west and north of the big pyramids were probably markets. The main avenue and its buildings were drained through an underground drainage system which carried rain water and waste off to a nearby river.

The big pyramids themselves represent mute testimonies of a social system which harnessed the labor of its members for gigantic religious constructions. The Pyramid of the Sun, 689 feet by 689 feet at the base and 210 feet high, contains about 1,300,000 cubic yards of earth. Its construction must have absorbed the labor of 10,000 people for 20 years.

Across the divide in the valley of Puebla rises another man-made mountain, the pyramid of Cholula. Its beginnings predate the Theocratic period; its core is a pyramid 55.5-58.8 feet high and covering 9.88 acres. The walls of this early structure were painted red, black, and yellow with representations of mythological insects. Four reconstructions and superimpositions by people closely related to the inhabitants of Teotihuacán brought the pyramid to its present size: 181 feet high and nearly 40 acres in extent, it is larger than the pyramid by which Cheops assured his immortality. The surfaces of the final structure were painted with dark rectangles. According to a tradition collected by the Spaniards the temple was dedicated to the worship of the god "9 Rain," probably a local incarnation of the Teotihuacán Tlaloc.

Who built Teotihuacán and Cholula? The builders probably did not belong to a single linguistic group. On the contrary, we may suppose that such large centers dominated an area inhabited by a number of different cultural and linguistic groups. Various sources identify the builders of Teotihuacán and Cholula with a group called Olmeca-Xicalanca. The Indian historian Chimalpain calls these Olmeca-Xicalanca *quiahuiztecos,* or "people of the rain," the Nahuatl cognate for the name by which the Mixtec call themselves —Ñusabi. It is increasingly likely that these Olmeca-Xicalanca were a Chocho-Popoloca or Mixtec-speaking group.

Beyond Cholula, Teotihuacán influence is associated with two other major centers. One of these, Kaminaljuyú, lies in the southeastern highlands, on the southwestern outskirts of Guatemala City. The other, Tajín, rises from the tropical rain forest, near the town of Papantla, in northern Veracruz. Kaminaljuyú has a history going back to the beginnings of seed-planting. By 500 B. C. it had achieved a peak of prosperity and population, a commercial influence, which it was never to experience again. Around A. D. 400 it was invaded and occupied by a group of people who brought with them Teotihuacán patterns of such faithfulness and completeness that we can easily assume they came from the main metropolis itself. The newcomers built a strongly nucleated ceremonial center and ball courts in an acropolis arrangement reminiscent of the Maya lowlands and took over control of trade relations within the region. Toward the end of their occupation, however, they seem to have severed connections with their mother city, and around A. D. 900 they abandoned the site in the face of military pressures which they could not withstand.

The center at Tajín seems to have been constructed some time around A. D. 600. Its core is formed by a pyramid, 82 feet high and 115 feet at the base; it differs from all other known Mesoamerican structures in that its surface is honeycombed with niches. These may be purely ornamental, or may represent symbolically the caves that harbor the "heart of the land." The surrounding site has been excavated only partially; much of it still lies under the tough tropical forest cover. Its strong Teotihuacán affiliations make it likely that Tajín was a colony of Teotihuacán satellites in the tropical lowlands. It was abandoned in A. D. 1200, in the wake of the disturbances which followed on the destruction of the Theocratic world.

Yet the local population continued to live in its vicinity, undisturbed by the fate of the political and religious nucleus. Surface sherds of all periods litter the surrounding countryside.

Teotihuacán influence, as measured by kinds of pottery and styles of mural decoration, also reached the great ceremonial center of Monte Albán in the valley of Oaxaca, where city-builders had carved a man-made platform, 3,117 feet long and 1,476 feet wide, out of the living rock, because they were not content to use the natural contour of the mountain. Here, 1,300 feet above the surrounding valley floor, they built great courtyards, surrounded by stairways and pyramids, tombs and courts, a great ceremonial complex perfectly oriented in space along a north-south axis. Westheim says that this architectural attempt "is basically and from its very beginning a departure from nature. The men who built it not only did not respect the lay of the land; they rejected it, they saw it as a part of chaos on which man must impose order." The function of this great ceremonial center remains a mystery. The large number of tombs suggests that the headmen of many communities lie entombed there. No source of water has been found to allow us to imagine how the inhabitants of the mountain assuaged their thirst. Perhaps they were the masters of a social system so tightly organized that they could rely on systematic deliveries of food and water from the three surrounding valleys. . . .

Contemporary with these highland and lowland Mexican sites are the Theocratic Maya sites of the tropical forest. The area in which Maya culture found its initial characterization is the north-central Petén, in which dense forest alternates with open savannas. The two main sites in this area are Tikal, probably the largest site in the Petén, and Uaxactún, perhaps the oldest. Tikal, "where the voices of the departed are heard," is situated in limestone country, 700 feet above sea level, on the shores of a lake now converted into a swamp. Its central precinct covers about a square mile; its core is formed by six great pyramids, the highest in the Maya area. Beyond the central precinct, suburbs extend for two to three miles in all directions. Its total population in A. D. 600 has been estimated at 100,000. Uaxactún, a few miles south of Tikal, is the site of the oldest Maya temple, the oldest dated monument in the Maya area, and the first site on which the appearance of the corbeled vault has been noted. The temple, called E-VII-sub, rescued from the depths of temple E-VII, which had covered it, was 27 feet high, faced with stucco, and provided with a ceremonial stairway flanked by huge masks representing the jaguar god. Four postholes on top mark the former location of a small sanctuary made of perishable materials. Stela 9, the oldest carved monolith in the Maya area, bears a date which corresponds to A. D. 328; the corbeled vaults are dated A. D. 278. The ceremonial district here was surrounded by settlement clusters. A survey carried out in 1937 revealed seventy-eight house mounds within a third of a mile around the ceremonial center. In both of these towns, the outlying settlements were connected to the ceremonial precinct by broad roads. Recent aerial photographs made in the course of explorations for oil have further revealed a great road in the northern part of the Petén area.

The cities of the central Petén seem to bear relationship to the settlements recently excavated in British Honduras. There settlements follow the course of the Belize River; house mounds cluster along the alluvial terraces in groups as small as five or six or as large as three hundred. Each of the clusters of a dozen or more houses maintained a small ceremonial center, while larger centers, such as Baking Pot or Benque Viejo, probably linked several settlement clusters.

Traveling westward across savannas and jungles, we encounter the cities of the Usumacinta River. Yaxchilán, together with its dependency of Bonampak, lies closest to the Petén. Piedras Negras occupies an intermediate position, while Palenque is the northwestern-most of the Usumacinta towns. In these cities, Maya sculpture and stucco-work reached its zenith. At the same time, they show traits which are non-Maya, which recall rather the highlands of Mexico. Piedras Negras is especially aberrant, in its reluctance to make use of the corbeled vault at the beginning of the Maya Classic; in its representation of human sacrifice, absent elsewhere in the Classic Maya area. And at Bonampak, Giles Healey encountered murals of enormous fluid power, depicting a raid and the ceremonial disposal of prisoners long before these customs were in general vogue in other parts of the Maya area.

Such highland ties we find also at Copán, the second largest Maya city in western Honduras. It lies in a fertile and well-watered valley, 1,800 feet above sea level, on the banks of the Copán River. Its acropolis, built under the direction of a group of Maya priests and their followers who immigrated sometime near the beginning of the ninth cycle of Maya calendar series, covers 12 acres. The large amount of utilitarian ware scattered in and about this area suggests that the residences of the common people lay in the shadow of the central ceremonial precinct. During its development, Copán was the scientific center of the Maya world. The astronomers of Copán worked out the length of the tropical year, first used or developed the eclipse tables, and worked out a calendar correction formula more accurate than our Gregorian leap year, all toward the end of the seventh century A. D. Two altars commemorate the meetings of this Copán Academy of Sciences: they show the assembled scientists facing toward a central date. Thompson suggests that the scientists came from all parts of the Maya domain. A figure wearing the ceremonial headdress of a bat may have come from the Chiapas mountains to repesent the Bat People (Tzotzil) at this scientific meeting. Certainly, shortly after the calendar reform at Copán, other centers accepted the innovation with an alacrity not commonly exhibited by rival bodies of professionals. But then this period around 700 may have witnessed not only the unification of the calendar, but also some form of political unification.

At the same time, new art forms, symbols of rulership, spread from the periphery of the Maya area across the entire Maya land; among these are the formal plumed headdress, the fringed sandal, the cuff-like wristlet, beaded plumes, and the manikin scepter. At Copán we find many representations of the Mexican Tlaloc. Are we dealing with a movement of political consolidation that had its origins outside the Maya area, even though it made use of traditional Maya forms? But near the end of the Classic period, Copán is abandoned suddenly. One day the town bustles with activity; the next day priests and commoners alike pack up and leave, and abandon their temples and houses to the jungle and to the jaguar.

Usually not included among major Maya centers, because they lagged behind the others in the refinement of their art, are Calakmul, Cobá, and Dzibalchultún. Calakmul, in southern Campeche, possesses with its 103 stelae more time markers than any other Maya site, though it lacks other monuments of artistic merit. Cobá is the earliest Theocratic center in northeastern Yucatán; its beginnings date back to A. D. 623. It lies amidst five small lakes, the largest of which is a mile long. Sixteen known causeways, each 15 feet wide, connected the town itself with outlying centers. The longest, over 60 miles long, linked Cobá with Yaxuna, not far from Chichén Itzá. Like other Theocratic Maya centers, both these towns are located in the tropical rain forest. Dzibalchultén, however, near modern Mérida, lies in the dry bush country so characteristic of northwestern Yucatán. Only now under excavation, it may well turn out to be the largest of all known Maya centers. Its size has been estimated at

20 square miles, 10 square miles of which was densely packed with temples and house platforms. Moreover, it was inhabited continuously from 1500 B. C. to the time of the Spanish Conquest. The continued study of its remains may well throw an entirely new light on the Theocratic period in the whole Maya-speaking area.

XIV / PREHISTORIC CULTURES OF THE AMERICAN SOUTHWEST

INTRODUCTION

The area that now constitutes the continental United States, like temperate Europe, was marginal to the early centers of civilization, and, although not immune to their influences, the native populations of the United Staes never attained the pinnacle reached by some of their Latin American neighbors. In this peripheral setting, however, two regions did see the formation of relatively complex agricultural societies—the Eastern Woodlands and the Southwest.

In the Southwest, domesticated plants were introduced, presumably from Mexico, a couple of thousand years before Christ. This eventually led to the establishment of sedentary communities such as the Pueblos that one can see there today. The nature of the prehistoric settlements, as well as their contents, implies fairly advanced social, economic, and religious organizations having exceedingly few traits of fully Mexican character. In spite of roughly similar adaptations, this area was not culturally uniform, for archaeologists have identified no less than four major traditions. The peak of these developments was probably between about A. D. 700 and 1300, when the incursion of nomadic peoples like the Navaho and Apache began to cause considerable strife and disorganization. It may be that drought and internal disruption also contributed to this decline.

◇   ◇   ◇

Archaeological interest in the southwestern part of the United States —that is, Arizona, New Mexico, and parts of Nevada, Utah and

From *Digging into History* by Paul S. Martin (Chicago Natural History Museum Popular Series, Anthropology, No. 38). Copyright © 1959 by the Chicago Natural History Museum. Reprinted by permission of the Chicago Natural History Museum.

Colorado—began in 1875 or thereabouts. At that time the country was being settled by cattlemen, sheepmen, and farmers. The large standing ruins that were fairly abundant in parts of Arizona, New Mexico, and Colorado naturally attracted the interest of lay workers as well as that of archaeologists. From about 1880 to 1910 many famous scientists visited the Southwest and described numerous sites and the Indians they saw there. From about 1875 to 1925, it was commonly believed by most laymen and most archaeologists that the entire area had been inhabited and developed by one group, the so-called Pueblo people. The great cliff-houses at Mesa Verde, the large, open D-shaped villages in Chaco Canyon, the famous villages in southwestern New Mexico that produced beautiful pottery, the great adobe houses of southern Arizona, the canals in that area, and all the villages and pueblos and ruins of all kinds up and down the Gila, the Salt, the Little Colorado, and the San Juan Rivers—all of these were supposed to have been the work of the Pueblo Indians. We now know that this was a very simplified picture of what had actually occurred. At the present time archaeologists recognize four major subdivisions and four major subcultures of the Southwest. Each of these major subdivisions and subcultures had characteristics of its own and for some time it was believed that each flourished independently. Recent work has shown that each did have its own individual characteristics, but that all of them are united in various subtle but tangible ways. All these four subcultures seem to have been motivated by similar impulses to change in more or less the same direction at about the same time. And all reached a climax about A. D. 1300. It is as if the area had been washed over several times by waves of similar cutlural influences.

The names of the four major subcultures are: (1) Anasazi, (2) Hohokam, (3) Mogollon, and (4) Patayan.

The Anasazi Culture

The word "Anasazi"—which is an Anglicized version of the Navaho term meaning "old people"—is the name now applied to Basketmakers, Cliff Dwellers, and Pueblo Indians. Anasazi, then, is the inclusive term.

The territory in which the Anasazi Indians lived from about the beginning of the Christian era is what is known today as the "Four-Corners" region. This region may be roughly described as northeastern Arizona, northwestern New Mexico, southeastern Utah and southwestern Colorado. Anasazi ruins are found from Flagstaff eastward to the Rio Grande River, but the concentration is mostly in the

"Four-Corners" area. Even today there are remnants of the Anasazi people living in or about the same area; for example, the Hopi Indians live in northeastern Arizona, the Zuñi Indians live in towns close to the Arizona-New Mexico border, and the Rio Grande Indians live in and around Albuquerque and Santa Fe. All of these present-day Indians have retained a remarkable degree of their ancient culture and the Zuñi and Hopi Indians are noted for their conservatism because they have effectively resisted the encroachments of our European civilization.

The Anasazi civilization which flourished on the Colorado plateau of the Intermontane division has been more intensively investigated and written about than any of the others. For fifty years, reports, monographs, articles, and stories have been pouring from the pens of various authors, and the literature is very voluminous. Therefore, I shall condense what I have to say about this culture. Briefly, it may be summed up as follows:

Taking Anasazi culture as a whole from beginning to end, without differentiating the time factors, we may say that its chief characteristics are (1) masonry; (2) agglomerations of houses, often several stories high (roughly similar to our clusters of rooms called apartment houses); (3) the *kiva,* or ceremonial underground chamber; (4) altars; (5) sand pantings (ritualistic scenes portrayed freehand with sands of various colors); (6) priestly offices; (7) elaborate rituals and symbolisms, some of which were secret and celebrated in the sanctuary (*kiva*) and many of which were held in the open for the enjoyment and inspiration of the entire village; (8) special public dances performed by katchinas or representatives of the gods to re-enact the Hopi beliefs concerning the origin of the tribe and to insure peace, prosperity, rainfall, good crops, tribal fertility, and health, and to express thankfulness for past favors; (9) probably mother-line descent; (10) textured or corrugated grayish cooking pottery; (11) decorated pottery with a gray or white background and designs in black paint; (12) decorated pottery of a polychrome and glazed decorated type.

The Anasazi culture, like the other three subcultures, grew by continuous transitions and additions and accretions from an ancient and widespread culture called the Desert Culture of the Great Basin (the Intermontane area). The Desert Culture came into existence some 11,000 years ago and monopolized most of the territory in the Great Basin—that it, from Oregon and Idaho southward through Nevada, Utah, and parts of California and Colorado, Arizona, and New Mexico—and extended into the northern part of Mexico. The

Great Basin area lies mostly within the sagebrush-juniper-pinyon zone, although there are good-sized regions of short desert grass and of pines, hemlocks, and spruce in the higher mountains. Parenthetically, it is interesting to note that today most of the area is occupied by peoples who speak dialects of the Uto-Aztecan language, including the modern Hopis, Pimas, Utes, Paiutes and Shoshones, and some of the Rio Grande Indians.

Most of the later and so-called higher developments of the Anasazi came to them from the Hohokam and Mogollon groups (see below), so that the climax that occurred about A. D. 1100 may be regarded as an accumulation of southern and possibly Mexican traits that were taken over by the Anasazi bit by bit—by trade, by drift, perhaps by war—and reworked to fit their ideas and cultural layout. In fact, much of the great efflorescence of culture that took place in the Hopi and Zuñi towns may be due to ideas conceived by the Mogollon peoples who were beginning to move up into the Hopi-Zuñi country around 1200 to 1300.

The Hohokam Culture

Now let us look briefly at the Hohokam culture. The civilization of the Hohokam Indians (Hohokam is an anglicized version of the Pima Indian term meaning "that which had perished"), like that of the Anasazi, was probably derived from a desert culture that was established some 11,000 years ago in the Intermontane region. The area of Hohokam specialization lay mostly along the Gila River and its tributaries in the southern half of Arizona—that is, in the desert regions of Phoenix and Tucson. Hohokam features and villages are found, however, far beyond this limited area. Certainly Hohokam traits spread as far north as the Flagstaff region and as far south as the international border—perhaps even farther.

As I stated above, the Gila-Salt River drainages, now known to be the homeland of the Hohokam, were formerly considered a part of the Puebloan Southwest. Prior to 1920 every archaeological site in the Southwest was dubbed "Cliff-dweller" or "Pueblo." In short, the Southwest was "the Pueblo area." A few imaginative archaeologists who heeded the evidence thought otherwise. The great contrast between the materials found in the Gila River desert ruins and those from the Plateau sites made them think that perhaps it was a bit "fishy" to lump together two obviously different groups. The trouble is that they had no concrete evidence on which to base sound deductions.

But, thanks to Gila Pueblo at Globe, Arizona (a privately endowed research institution, supported and directed by Mr. and Mrs. H. S. Gladwin, but now dissolved, alas), work was carried on in the fall, winter, and spring seasons. Due entirely to the dogged persistence of the Gladwins and their staff, the Gila desert area and the territories surrounding it—east, west, south, and north—were systematically explored. By 1928 or 1929, the staff of Gila Pueblo knew for certain that the Gila-Salt River drainages and the desert area were *not* parts of the Pueblo area and that the archaeological remains represented a separate entity or subculture. Thus they discovered the Hohokam civilization. The Pueblo "one world" was shattered, and about 1930, or thereabouts, Southwestern archaeologists conceded that the Southwest geographical area embraced several prehistoric civilizations. The acceptance of the Mogollon culture as another entity was delayed for several years. Scientific explorations and excavations in Hohokam sites has not yet been extensive, but each year sees more work done in this interesting civilization. Enough is now known, however, so that we can describe confidently the highlights of the Hohokam subculture. The largest site, Snaketown, was investigated for several seasons by the staff of Gila Pueblo.

If we take the Hohokam civilization from early to late (from about the beginning of the Christian era to about A. D. 1400) without regard to time periods, we may list its traits as follows: (1) pithouses—structures with the floor below the surface of the ground, and the roof made of brush and mud (note: storied clusters of houses were never built by the Hohokam); (2) villages composed of scattered houses, but no towns; (3) compound walls around some of the later villages; (4) irrigation ditches for taking water from the Gila and its tributaries to the fields (without irrigation of some type agriculture would have been impossible in this desert); (5) pottery made by the paddle and anvil process instead of the coiling process used by the Anasazi and Mogollon Indians, and manufactured in such a way as to produce a red ware or a buff type with designs in red paint (red-on-buff ware); (6) etched shell ornaments; (7) excellent stone carvings; (8) well-made projectile points; (9) stone axes of fine quality, the handles of which were fastened to a three-quarter groove (a groove that runs around three sides of the tool); (10) rituals that were probably simpler than and different from the complex ones of the Anasazi; (11) ball courts in which a kind of ceremonial basketball game was played; (12) small kivas; (13) medicine men rather than priests and a priesthood; (14) father-line descent; (15) perhaps some aggressiveness or warlike expansive traits.

What became of the Hohokam peoples after A. D. 1400? Did they and their civilization perish from the face of the earth? Several anthropologists have conjectured that the modern Pima Indians who live in southern Arizona are the cultural descendants of the Hohokam Indians, and recent work by the Amerind Foundation of Arizona has strengthened this hypothesis. If this is so, then we have an unbroken continuity of the Hohokam culture from a desert base of about 11,000 years ago, through the Hohokam civilization itself, which surely came into being by the beginning of the Christian era, right down to the present Pima or related Indians. In other words, the Hohokam civilization faltered and changed its course and thereby lost much of its polish about A. D. 1400, but it did not perish.

There are many differences between the traits of the Anasazi and Hohokam Indians. Chief among these are: For the Anasazi: masonry; storied houses with clustered rooms; "towns"; the kiva; priests and altars; grayish plain or black-on-white pottery and, later, black-on-yellow or orange wares and glazed paint wares. For the Hohokam: lack of masonry; pit-houses; small groups of houses; the compound; the ball court; shamans rather than a priesthood; the red-on-buff pottery that cannot compare for general excellence with the Anasazi ceramics.

The Mogollon culture, as noted above, was also discovered by the staff of Gila Pueblo in 1934 or thereabouts. The first excavations in a Mogollon site were made by Dr. Emil W. Haury, whose publication is now a landmark in the archaeological works of the Southwest. But for a long time conservative archaeologists refused to accept the Mogollon civilization as a separate entity. Now, however, this culture stands on its own feet and has been accepted by archaeologists throughout the world. No more at this point will be said about it.[1]

The Patayan Culture

The fourth subculture of the Southwest is called Patayan (with accent on the second syllable). It is the least studied and described of the four principal civilizations of the Southwest. The name, Patayan, is taken from the Yuman language and the word means "ancient people." The dates for this culture are at the moment tentatively placed at A. D. 700 to 1100. A few good excavations have been carried on in Patayan sites, and from these studies, together with the

[1] The remainder of *Digging into History* is devoted to the Mogollon culture [*ed.*].

vast amount of information gleaned from "surveys" carried on by the Museum of Northern Arizona, we can derive some tentative conclusions.

The Patayans are believed to be the cultural, physical and linguistic ancestors of the present-day Havasupai, Walapai, or Yuman tribes, who occupy much of the same territory on the Colorado River plateau and in the canyons of that river as did the ancient Patayan. In ancient times these Indians lived not only along the Colorado River, but also as far east as the Verde River at Flagstaff and south approximately as far as 34° N. Lat.

The ancient economy of the Patayan Indians were probably based on agriculture plus some hunting and food-gathering. Thus it resembles the other three subcultures. Houses were of several types and were probably occupied seasonally—possibly a snug type of earth-covered, dome-shaped house for winter habitation, and a "shade" structure for summer usage. Villages as such did not exist; houses were scattered singly over a general area. Stone tools such as the lower and upper parts of corn-grinding stones (metates and manos), projectile points, knives and scrapers occur but were not of noteworthy workmanship. No religious structures or burials have been found.

In general, one senses that the Patayans farmed sporadically and where they could, expressed little interest in manufacturing tools of bone and stone, made few or no ornaments, and left behind no ceremonial structures of the type that is usually regarded as evidence of a visible ritual, such as the Anasazi possessed. This does not necessarily mean a lack of religious ideas; perhaps their regligion was expressed in other ways. All in all, the Patayan culture shows some resemblances to, or at least an indirect relationship with, the ancient and widespread cultures of the Great Basin. Here again it resembles the other three subcultures. There are also connections with later Anasazi civilizations, but these are regarded as due to borrrowing.

This concludes the brief discussion of the [Anasazi, Hohokam, and Patayan] subcultures of the southwestern part of the United States. I have stressed their differences in order to make clear to the reader that each has reality and that each can be distinguished from the other. Now I wish to point out the hypothesis that these four subcultures are intimately related in one way or another even though each has its own distinct flavor. That is why I prefer the term "subculture" for each one, so that the emphasis is placed on the fact that the Southwest is one large "culture area." A culture area may be roughly defined as a geographical region that embraces similar or related culture traits or elements, similar patterns and drifts that must be regarded as having depth in time. The Southwest culture area appears, then, to comprise four related but consistently distinctive culture types or subcultures.

Thus I believe that the Southwest can be regarded or characterized as a natural culture area that is a distinctive one. The four subcultures, considered collectively, certainly stand in stark contrast to those of the west, north, and east. This concept emphasizes the similarities that exist among the four local subcultures among which there has been an interchange of cultural factors and ideas. By this concept we sweep aside the artificial boundaries that archaeologists have thought up between the various groups (Anasazi, Hohokam, and the like), and point out that there probably was a large degree of mobility and interchange of ideas throughout the entire Southwest in all times—that is, from about 11,000 years ago down to the moment. That is what I mean by time depth.

INTRODUCTION

By approximately A.D. 800 the Mississippian cultures, considered by some archaeologists the peak of cultural development in this country before Columbus, appeared in the southeastern United States and the Mississippi Valley. These late prehistoric and early historic maize-cultivators were very Mexican in nature, and their palisaded towns were built around a plaza associated with truncated earthen temple mounds. Craftsmanship in ceramics, featherwork, shellwork, and stonework was excellent, and we know from early European accounts that many of the final Mississippians were on the threshold of urbanization. People such as the Natchez of Mississippi had civil and war chiefs, priests, and even slaves. It was in these cultures that Mexican influence reached a climax, and how much further this would have progressed were it not for European intervention one can only surmise.

The highest level of prehistoric cultural development before the Mississippian period was among the Hopewell, or Middle Woodland, Indians of the Midwest, who between about 500 B. C. and A. D. 500 constructed immense earthworks and burial mounds. Although there may well have been some stimuli from Mexican cultures, Hopewellian accomplishments seem to have been more or less indigenous. In the settlements, and especially in the burial mounds, are found very refined works in stone, ceramics, and copper displaying craftsmanship seldom surpassed in any prehistoric period in the United States. Indeed, the quality of these artifacts and the wide array of materials employed have led to suggestions that the Hopewell maintained specialized craftsmen and sent out regular trading parties to obtain Gulf of Mexico seashells, Lake Superior copper,

157

and Rocky Mountain obsidian and grizzly bear teeth. Moreover, although the basis of the economy is supposed by most to have been the cultivation of maize, there seems to be more direct evidence of intensive hunting and collecting activities.

◇   ◇   ◇

The Hopewell Indians in Ohio lived mainly along the major rivers forming a part of the Ohio River drainage system. Many of their important sites are in the Ross County area in the valley of the Scioto or its tributaries. Other occupation centers were in the Great Miami, the Little Miami, and the Muskingum valleys. Evidences of related Hopewellian people are present in the adjacent states of Indiana, Kentucky, Pennsylvania, and Michigan and in other regions of the Eastern states. In physical type, the Hopewell peoples in Ohio were predominantly a longheaded group pertaining to the Sylvid classification of the Eastern Woodlands. One-fourth of the skulls show bifrontal deformation and a few occipital deformation. Diseased bones indicate that they were subject to dental caries, apical abscesses, arthritis, and perhaps syphilis.

The Hopewellian people in Ohio were the "Great Earthwork Builders," erecting enclosures of two general types, the geometrical earthworks and the hill top enclosures or "forts." The former, located in the valleys, include circles, rectangles, octagons, and combinations of these forms. At the larger sites, such geometrical enclosures are often connected by long parallel walls which evidently served as passageways. The walls of the earthworks, some with interior ditches, vary from several feet up to sixteen or more feet in height and often are broken by a number of openings or "gateways." Burial mounds are usually associated with the enclosures, often being located within them. They vary considerably in shape and size, ranging from small sub-conical or elongate mounds to large elongated mounds up to thirty feet in height and two hundred and forty feet long. Earthworks may enclose from ten to fifteen acres to over a hundred acres. Usually there are depressions near the earthworks from which the builders dug earth for their construction. Among some of the well-known sites of this kind are the Hopewell, Newark, Marietta, Seip, Mound City, Turner, Harness, and the Tremper earthworks.

Richard G. Morgan, "Outline of Cultures in the Ohio Region." From *Archaeology of Eastern United States*, ed. J. B. Griffin (Chicago: University of Chicago Press, 1952), pp. 88-92.

These geometrical enclosures were used as centers by the Hopewell peoples for social, religious, and burial purposes. Their sacred character is testified to by the achieving of privacy by walls and connecting passageways, their symbolical form, and their use for the burial of important personages in the group. This latter fact is supported by the evidence of extremely elaborate burial practices, the placing of great ceremonial offerings or "sacrifices" in the burial mounds, and the final erection of large mounds over certain of the sacred structures. It is likely that the chief-priests of the tribe lived at the earthworks and that the important burials and offerings pertained to them and their families.

The second kind of earthworks is typified by Fort Ancient, a hill-top enclosure, on the Little Miami River in Warren County, Ohio. Sites of this type, located mainly in southwestern Ohio, are characterized by earthen or stone walls enclosing the relatively level tops of hills isolated from the surrounding country side by steep sided valleys or ravines. Burial mounds were built within and adjacent to the hill-top enclosures in a few cases, and they have features such as parallel walls, paved ways and burial mounds which seem to have had ceremonial functions. Although the hill-top enclosures have been termed "forts," it is evident that they were used as ceremonial centers as well as for defense.

Since the Hopewell Culture in Ohio has been mainly defined from artifacts and other traits associated with the burial cult, a well-rounded picture of the village and everyday life of these people cannot be given. However, village refuse in the mounds and earthworks, and beneath and around them, gives abundant evidence that at least some of the Hopewell people lived at the sites of the major enclosures. Sites showing thick deposits of village debris have not so far been found in Ohio.

Pottery vessels were made for both utilitarian and ceremonial usages, but as they were rarely buried with the dead, few whole ones are found. A number of forms were made, including jars, bowls, platters and plates. The bottoms of the pots were rounded or flattened, and a few of the smaller vessels were made with four conical-shaped legs. All were without handles. Tempering material was either grit or limestone, with 80 per cent of the sherds having grit and about 19 per cent limestone, the remainder being sand or clay-tempered. All are gray or buff in color. Ordinary containers had cord-wrapped paddle impressions on their exterior surfaces or were plain. Sixty-four per cent of all sherds are cord-marked and twenty-three per cent are plain.

The finer or ceremonial vessels were all decorated by various stamping, incising, and cord-impressing techniques. The upper rim was usually thickened and decorated with cross-hatched incised lines bordered by a row of hemiconical punctate impressions. The body surface was covered with an over-all stamped design, or by curvilinear zones or bands with stamped impressions set off from plain smooth areas by incised lines. Some of the smaller vessels were made with four body-lobes with bird designs on them. Ceramic artifacts include platform pipes, button cores for covering with copper, beads, circular ear ornaments, and human figurines.

The Hopewell people, on the whole, produced the best made tools, weapons and ornaments of any group in the Eastern United States. A study of their artifacts indicates that they had specialized craftsmen, for some objects required skills which could only be acquired by long practice. They worked not only in stone, bone, and shell but extensively in wood, hides, feathers, and other perishable substances. When certain materials or natural objects were scarce, they would imitate them in other substances.

Their projectile points, knives, scrapers, and drills were chipped largely from local flint. There is strong evidence that the atlatl or spear-thrower was in common use, although they may also have had the bow and arrow. The large size of most of the points, the occurrence of certain stone artifact types which seem to be atlatl weights, and the presence of what has been interpreted as an effigy atlatl in mica, all point to the use of the spear-thrower. Furthermore, several antler objects were found which are considered to be atlatl hooks. Projectile points are mainly corner-notched, side-notched and stemmed for hafting, although some blades were made in leaf-shaped or triangular forms. Very large blades of several forms, evidently ceremonial in nature, were chipped from obsidian, quartz, or flint. Some cone-shaped points were rolled from copper, while others were made of antler tines. Curved and straight bladed knives were made, and small flake knives with razor-sharp edges were struck from flint cores. Flint scrapers were made in ovoid, rectanguloid, and notched forms, and flint drills were of the plain or notched-for-hafting types. A few chisels, some with bone handles, were pounded out of copper and meteoritic iron.

Axes of the ungrooved type (no doubt hafted in a wooden handle) were pecked from hard stones and polished. Axes and adzes were also hammered from copper nuggets and pieces of meteoritic iron. Hammerstones and abrading stones were used, but stone mortars and pestles were very rare. Bowls and cups were very rarely made out of stone, but charred fragments of wooden bowls and other objects hint at an extensive use of wood. Containers were also fashioned from conch shells (mainly Busycon perversum) and from the carapace of turtles. Bone objects include needles, awls, flint-chipping tools, skewers, and pins, spatulas, and digging implements. Spoons were cut from fresh-water mussel shells.

The Hopewell people made a great variety of ornamental objects, with beads being the most common form. Beads cut from fresh-water mussel shells and marine snail shells occur in great quantities with burials. A common form was disk-shaped, but barrel-shaped, globular, and cylindrical beads were also used. Beads made from Marginella and Anculosa shells were common, and drilled fresh-water pearls were used abundantly as grave offerings. Beads of stone, copper, bone, and seeds were also used. Animal canine teeth were drilled for pendants, as were bird and animal claws. Bear canines were sometimes elaborately carved, and occasionally set with pearls. A few perforated alligator and shark teeth were used, with the possibility that the latter may have formed the cutting edges of swords and clubs.

Ornaments worn directly on the person included earrings, bracelets, headdresses, combs, and finger rings. The common form of ear ornament was the spool-shaped one of copper, which was sometimes overlaid with silver or meteoritic iron. Finely made circular ear ornaments of stone and wood were also used, some of which were perforated, possibly for the attachment of small pendants. Bracelets of copper were not common, while copper finger rings were very rare. Copper breastplates with two holes for attachment were common, some being decorated with scrolls or bosses, or cut in the form of birds (usually the hawk). Carved tortoise shell combs and copper rods were used in the hair. Copper plates served as foundations for the headdresses. Some were plain, some had cut-out designs, and others were set with copper antlers. Impressions of fabric and feathers on the copper and the presence of pearls and mica designs indicate some of the headdresses were elaborate.

Pendants and plummets were made from stone, copper, bone and shell. Button-like objects of wood or stone covered with copper were fairly common. Designs cut from sheets of copper or mica were made in the forms of animals, humans, birds, fish, crescents, circles, triangles, scrolls, and swastikas. Usually they were perforated for attachment to clothing. Stone gorgets perforated with one or two holes for suspension, include rectanguloid, expanded-center, reel-shaped, and diamond-shaped forms. The reel-shaped form was also made of copper, and the rectanguloid form sometimes of copper, bone, shell, or tortoise shell. Circular gorgets and disks were made from shell, wood, stone, bone, copper, and iron. Boatstones, perhaps used as atlatl weights, were usually made of stone. Some represented birds and animals, including the hawk and the mythical horned serpent.

Animal and human jaws were cut and perforated for suspension, with some of the former having incised and painted designs. Hollow copper turtle effigies containing pebbles served as rattles on a leather belt. Human parietal bones were cut into circular gorgets and incised with conventional bird designs. Animal long bones were sometimes incised with expertly executed designs in the form of animals, birds, geometric figures and mythological beings. Other ornamental objects comprise incised spadefish bones, bones banded with copper, hawk skulls, a tablet with a rattlesnake design, and oval and rectanguloid stone tablets. It is likely that some of these were used by medicine men and formed the contents of the medicine bags. Copper noses were used in connection with three burials. A few small sheets of gold indicate that this material was known, but was extremely rare. Musical instruments include rattles, and triple conjoined-tubes (of reed, wood, or bone covered with copper, silver, or meteoritic iron) which are apparently pan pipes.

Tobacco, judging from the great quantities of pipes in ceremonial offerings, played an important part in the ceremonial life of the Hopewell people. Their pipes, usually carved from a hard flint clay (Ohio pipestone), were of the platform type with either a curved or straight base. Some were plain, while others had their bowls expertly carved in the forms of various birds and animals native to the region. In all cases the animal faces the smoker. It is noteworthy that most of the effigy pipes were found in two great ceremonial offerings. Tubular and modified pipes were very rare.

The Hopewell people had a well-developed weaving art. Cloth preserved by copper objects shows they used the techniques of plain plaiting, twilled plaiting, looping, plain twining, and twilled twining. Thread was made from plant fibers as well as from rabbit hair. Some of the weaving may have been done on a simple loom, although there is no tangible evidence of such implements. Twine served for a variety of uses, and mats, bags, and baskets were woven. Some fabrics were decorated in color with painted geometrical designs.

From pottery figurines and designs depicting the human figure, light is thrown upon their manner of dress and personal adornment.

Women wore wrap-around skirts and footwear of woven grass. Their hair was parted in the center and gathered into a knot at the back of the head. Men wore breechcloths, belts, and moccasins of Algonquian type to which short leggings were fitted. Their hair was worn in several styles, in one of which, a knot was formed in the center of the forehead. In another, it was gathered into a hairnet, and in some cases they shaved the sides of the head leaving a ridge of hair from front to back in the center. Their ears were pierced and distended for the insertion of several types of ear ornaments. Facial painting or tattooing, or perhaps both, were practiced. Garments were made of skin, fur, and fabric, although little may be said of the form they took.

The Hopewell people had the most elaborate burial customs of any prehistoric group in the region, or perhaps in North America. Their ceremonies took place within their geometrical enclosures, and interment of the dead was made in structures within or adjacent to them. Post-mold patterns beneath the mounds indicate that circular, oval, and elongated rectanguloid structures were built in which burial rites were conducted and tombs placed. Large wooden posts were placed in separately dug holes to form the sides of the structures which varied in size from about fifteen or twenty feet across to over fifty. Some of the elongate forms were as much as two hundred feet in length. Some of the smaller structures were houses, judging from the arrangement of fireplaces and the presence of post-molds which may indicate roof supports. The great size of other structures would seem to show that they were not roofed; however, some were divided into smaller compartments which may have been covered. Characteristically, these "houses" had level sand-covered floors of clay, compacted by intentional puddling or by long continued use. Their burial practices may be summarized as follows. Upon the death of an individual who was to be buried in the flesh, the body was dressed in the finest garments and ornaments and placed in an extended position on the back in a charnel house upon a rectangular burial platform on the floor. This puddled clay platform was surrounded by a log tomb from one to three logs in height, and covered by logs or slabs, with layers of bark often placed beneath and over the logs. The logs were held in place with vertical stakes or stone slabs. Implements and ornaments, usually ceremonially "killed" or broken to release their "spirits," were then placed in the grave. Artifacts were often placed symmetrically around the rectangular tomb, while in other cases burials were encircled by ornaments or small stones. A copper ear ornament was commonly placed at each hand and a conch shell at each corner of the platform.

Burials were sometimes accompanied by thousands of pearl or shell beads, and dozens of other ornaments and implements. Red ocher was strewn over the body and artifacts, or applied directly to the bones, a fact showing that the bodies sometimes laid in state long enough for the flesh to have decayed. In some cases as many as six bodies were placed in one large tomb. Separate skulls placed in some graves are considered to have been those of revered ancestors, since they conform in physical type to those of the main burials. Extended burials in the flesh were also placed in stone-slab graves. Flexed burials occurred at one site and bundle burials at another, the latter custom being indicative of some form of reburial.

Cremation was practiced more than burial in the flesh, with over three-fourths of all burials being of that type. Cremation took place in rectangular basins of puddled clay which had sloping sides and flat bottoms. They were from three to five inches deep and varied in length from three to over ten feet. Some show evidence of long and repeated use, and in rare cases they were used for depositories for the cremated remains and accompanying artifacts. A few bodies were cremated in the flesh, but most cremations were apparently of dismembered defleshed skeletons. This argues for a practice in which the bodies were exposed for a considerable period of time, perhaps on platforms or scaffolds, as among some historic tribes. After cremation the charred bones and ashes were deposited on prepared platforms surrounded by log tombs. Some tombs were used for the ashes of one person, while in others the remains of a number of cremated bodies were placed.

Artifacts were burned with the body or placed with the ashes at the time of deposition on the prepared platforms. Large offerings were also placed in special depositories separate from the tombs or upon wooden platforms. Certain "houses" or compartments were used for cremation, some for tombs and others for the storage of ceremonial objects. Well-made circular fire basins of puddled clay may represent the sites of ceremonial fires. After a lapse of time, individual tombs were covered with small mounds. In a few cases' "canopies" of woven fabric were placed over these mounds and pinned down with bone skewers, while others were covered with layers of sand or gravel. Following this, the wooden structures forming the walls of the houses were burned. Earth was then piled over the small mounds forming a larger mound which took the outline of the pre-mound wooden structure. In some cases, the larger primary and secondary mounds were encircled by retaining walls and coverings of stone and gravel, with a gravel layer frequently extending over the entire mound. When the enclosures became filled with burial mounds they were apparently abandoned in favor of new sites.

The Hopewell people apparently lived in permanent villages.[1] Their large earthworks, with all the sustained labor they imply, point to this conclusion. The fact that they practiced agriculture, raising corn and no doubt its associated plants, likewise indicates a nonnomadic people. Hunting was probably important, while gathering of wild foods played only a secondary role. A people capable of building the great earthworks and who had such elaborate burial customs must have had a well-developed social organization. There may have been totemic clans, for certain animals and birds were used extensively for ceremonial motifs. Sites of the Hopewell culture by no means have complete cultural identity. Some differences may no doubt be attributed to local variations at a given time level, while others may indicate that some sites are older.

[1] Some archaeologists now believe they lived in smaller, scattered groups which cooperated in the construction of mounds and earthworks [ed.].

XVI / ON THE NATURE OF CIVILIZATION

INTRODUCTION

We have seen that the archaeologist, wishing to learn more of pre-historic humanity than bones and artifacts alone can tell him, often attempts to reconstruct the life and ways of earlier men through comparison with the nonliterate cultures and societies of today's world. Anthropologists shudder at the use of the term "Stone Age" for those who continue to follow a nonindustrialized, nonurban mode of existence today, since their histories are equally as long as our own. There are, however, obvious parallels in technology and economy between present-day and ancient nonliterate groups, and most anthropologists agree that certain similarities in patterns of social organization and, in general, outlook on life would therefore be likely. Subsistence agriculture or hunting and food-gathering tend to place restrictions on the size and make-up of social groups, and a limited technology usually means that many aspects of the universe are accounted for in supernatural rather than in scientific terms.

These are relatively simple conclusions, but sometimes one must go beyond purely technological considerations. This is especially true when we delve into the origins of civilization, probably the most complicated problem with which the archaeologist must cope. Urbanization means much more than merely the expansion of a village into a city, for radical changes are wrought in the whole spectrum of human relationships and the integration of society. By contrasting peasant and urban communities of the past with those of the present, a noted anthropologist comes to grips with the conse-quence of the "urban revolution" and how these affected mankind.

◇   ◇   ◇

What can be said that is general and true about the condition of mankind before civilization? The question is directed to a time from five to six thousand years ago. At that time human populations were to be found on all the world's continents, with the possible exception of Australia. Greenland had not yet been invaded by man, and some of the islands of the Pacific were as yet without human occupants. But there were people in a great many widely scattered parts of the habitable earth, not very many of them in any one place, and not very many of them altogether. No city had yet been built anywhere.

The question is whether anything can be said, with show of reason and evidence, about *all* the human beings that were there then, whether they lived in the arctic or in the tropics, whether they hunted, fished, or farmed, and whatever may have been the color of their skins, the languages they spoke, or the particular beliefs and customs that they had. The question demands a positive characterization of their manner of life. The description should be more than a mere statement of the things that those early men did not have that we today do have. It should say: this is what they did; this is how they felt; this is the way the world looked to them.

The question, so understood, appears to require more than can be provided from trustworthy evidence, but I do not think that it really does. It can be answered from two sources of information. The archaeologists dig up the material things that men of those times made and used, and from these things draw reasonable inferences about their manner of life. And, secondly, the ethnologists tell us a good deal about the ways of life of those people who until recent times have remained uncivilized: the primitive, the preliterate—or, to use the old-fashioned terms—the savage and the barbaric peoples. To learn what precivilized men were like, we may look to the accounts of the remains of ancient camps and settlements unaffected by cities, either because they were there before there were any cities anywhere, or because they stood remote and unreached by ancient cities already arisen. And also we may look to what has been written in great detail about many hundreds of present-day tribes and bands and villages, little communities of the never civilized. I do not assume that these latter people have experienced no changes in the several thousands of years since the first cities were built. The particular thoughts and beliefs of the present-day preliterates have

Robert Redfield, *The Primitive World and Its Transformations* (Ithaca, N.Y.: Cornell University Press, 1953). Copyright 1953 by Cornell University. Reprinted by permission of Cornell University Press.

probably changed a good deal during many hundreds of generations. The customs of these people are not "earlier" than is our
own civilization, for they have had as long a history as have we. But
what I do assert is that the surviving primitive peoples have remained substantially unaffected by civilization. Insofar as the conditions of primitive life remain—in the smallness of the community,
and in its isolation and nonliteracy—so, too, the kind of thoughts
and beliefs, however changed in specific content, remain of a kind
characteristic of primitive society. That there is such a kind is evi-
denced to us from the fact that we can generalize as to this manner
of thought and belief from the surviving primitive peoples, in the
face of the very great variety of content of thought and belief which
these exhibit. These surviving primitive peoples provide us with
instances of that general and primordial kind of human living
which it is my immediate purpose to describe.

Now it is fortunate for the present enterprise that these two
sources of information, the archaeological and the ethnological,
supplement each other. Where the former is weak, the latter is
strong; and where the ethnologist may be insufficiently impressed by
the influence of technology on the manner of life of a human community, the archaeologist can hardly fail to be impressed. This is
what he sees: the material things. Moreover, of the many meanings
which are locked in the artifacts that ancient peoples made, it is
those meanings which relate to practical action, especially the getting of food, which communicate themselves most readily to the
archaeologist who finds them. A Plains Indian medicine bundle or
an Australian totemic design as an archaeological object by itself
would convey only a little of the very great deal which the ethnologist who can talk to a living Indian or Australian can find out that it
means. So the archaeologist's view of the manner of life of the precivilized peoples will emphasize the practical aspects of living and
the material influences on change. An archaeologist should make a
little effort to lean deliberately away from a materialist view of
human life and a conception of history in simple terms of economic
determinism. His work inclines him toward it. On the other hand,
the ethnologist is often in a position where he can find out little or
nothing of the history of the people he is studying, as they have
written nothing down about it, having no means to do so; and so it
may sometimes appear to him that they are to be explained chiefly
in terms of the kinds of marriage choices he finds them making
when he finds them, or the potlatches they give. In the absence of a
history, the way the material conditions of living limited that peo-

ple here or gave them a chance to develop something there may not be apparent.

Archaeologist and ethnologist, however, do often talk to each other, and indeed in some cases are the same person. So the separation of work, the difference in emphasis, is not so great as I have perhaps made it sound. In the attempt to characterize the precivilized manner of life, I will begin by following Childe, an archaeologist. Professor Childe is interested in the effects on human development of changes in the technology by which food is produced. He makes a separation of importance between that period in human history when men were hunters and fishers only (savagery), and that period when men had learned how to be agriculturalists or animal breeders (barbarism). The change from the one kind of life to the other he calls a revolution, "the food-producing revolution."

The discovery of how to produce food was, of course, of enormous importance in human history, and it is not too much to call it a revolution and to group it, as Childe does, with the "urban revolution," when civilization came into being, and with the industrial revolution of modern times. Yet certain qualifications or additions need to be made. It has been pointed out that the food-producing revolution was the more notable event in that from the condition of food-collecting one could not predict that food-producing would be achieved, but that when once food production had increased human population and made leisure possible, civilization was bound to come about. And it is also necessary to recognize that some of the changes characteristic of each stage may have taken place, in one community or another, before the revolution in technology that Childe stresses had occurred there. Thus we know that a sedentary village life is possible to a people who know nothing of agriculture or animal husbandry. The fishing Indians of our Northwest coast lived a village life and developed certain aspects of their culture very highly. In prehistoric times there existed on the Scandinavian coast sessile communities, quite comparable with Neolithic farmers in the village character of life, with pottery and the polishing of flint, but without crops or herds. Also, it is not unlikely that with the advent of agriculture there began some of those changes which we are able to see only when cities and writing have made them visible to us. . . . As the changes in technology, so also the changes in the human mind which are the subject of these pages may have well begun before the urban revolution, even before the food-producing revolution.

Nevertheless, within the wide generalizations that I am here attempting, the food-producing revolution and the urban revolution may be considered as two parts of one great transformation. To one interested in changes in human habits and capacities of mind, the urban revolution is the more important part, for it is with the coming of city life that we are able to see novel and transforming attitudes taken toward life and the universe. . . . The question as to the relative importance of Childe's two first revolutions may be set aside with this statement: the food-producing revolution was perhaps the turning point in the human career, but it was through the urban revolution that the consequences of the turn were realized.

Now let us attempt a characterization of mankind in precivilized times. Let us begin with the simple statement that in the primary condition of mankind the human community was small. As Childe says, writing of the food-collecting period, hunters and vegetable-food collectors usually live in small roving bands. Even the more stable settlement of Pacific coast Indian fishing people, of recent times exceptionally well provided with food, includes hardly more than thirty occupied houses and several hundred people. Nor does the immediate transition to food-producing increase substantially the size of the community, now a group of farmer's huts or a center of cattle raising. . . . Certain food-producing town centers well on the way to civilization do give indication of larger populations, but hunters' band or food producers' settlements are alike in general contrast to the far-larger community which was the ancient city with its seven thousand to twenty thousand inhabitants. What is here worth emphasizing is that until the rise of civilization mankind lived in communities so small that every adult could, and no doubt did, know everybody else.

These communities were isolated from one another. Again Childe gives us to understand that the change in this regard with the coming of agriculture was a change in some degree, but at first not a radical change. Throughout both Paleolithic and Neolithic times each little group was largely self-contained and self-supported, as the surviving primitive societies, whether hunters or growers of vegetable or animal food, are largely self-contained and self-supported. The trade that occurred in Paleolithic times was chiefly trade in nonessentials; with Neolithic times the trade intensified and included some staple commodities, such as stone for querns and flint for hand axes. But the trade did not greatly limit the essential separateness of the local community. The isolation of the Neolithic settlement continued into the medieval English village. Villages of primitives or peasants today are still relatively isolated, and, on the whole, when such people have more than casual association with outsiders, it is with people who are much like themselves, in neighboring bands or settlements that are like their own community.

So we may characterize mankind in its primary condition as living in small and isolated communities. These communities were of course without writing. I do not say more of this absence of literacy and literature; its importance as a criterion of primitive as contrasted with civilized living is familiar. To these qualities others may be added. The precivilized community was composed of one kind of people. If this fact is not to be deduced from the archaeologist's data, it follows from what we know of isolated primitive communities seen today. Small and isolated communities are intimate communities; people come to have the same ways of doing things; they marry with and live almost entirely with others like them in that community.

Next we may say that the members of the precivilized community had a strong sense of group solidarity. No doubt they thought of themselves as naturally belonging together, and so far as they were aware of people different from themselves, they thought their own ways to be better than those of the ways of others. . . .

Let us follow Professor Childe further in his characterization of precivilized man. We see that now he must make increasing use of reasonable deduction and of the evidence from ethnology. He tells us that in the precivilized community there were no full-time specialists. He asserts this for the reason that in communities with simple hunting or even farming "there simply will not be enough food to go round unless every member of the group contributes to the supply." In the primitive societies of the present day there are rarely full-time specialists. So the assumption is fairly well founded that in the early condition of mankind what men did was customarily different from what women did, but what one man did was much like what another did. There were men with special skills at activities carried on by all men, and there were probably shamans or other part-time practitioners in the spiritual and healing arts. Differences among individuals with respect to the depth of understanding of cosmogonic and religious ideas may have been very considerable; this is a matter to which we shall recur on a later page. But, on the whole, all men shared the same essential knowledge, practiced the same arts of life, had the same interests and similar experiences.

Yet another characteristic of precivilized living may be asserted. Within those early communities the relationships among people were primarily those of personal status. In a small and intimate community all people are known for their individual qualities of personality. Few or no strangers take part in the daily life. So men and women are seen as persons, not as parts of mechanical operations, as city people see so many of those around them. Indeed, this disposition to see what is around one as human and personal like oneself is not, in precivilized or primitive society, limited to people; a great deal of what we call "nature" is more or less so regarded. The cosmos is personal and human-like.

Also in this connection it may be said that the grouping of people within the primitive community is one that depends on status and on role, not on mere practical usefulness. There are fathers, or older people, or shamans, or priests; each such kind of person is accorded prestige. In civilized societies the network of relationships of utility—the numbers and kinds of people who produce goods and services are so great and are at such remote distances—that many of the relationships that keep people provided with what they use are not involved in status at all, for those who use the goods. In primitive societies the status relationships are universal and dominant; the exceptions to be made would be those relatively few that arise out of trade with foreign communities.

Furthermore, in this personal universe where categories of relationships involve status, the forms and groupings of kinship provide the basic classifications. The original human society was one of kinsmen. Childe speaks of the "sentiment of kinship" which in considerable part held the group together. Within the precivilized society, it is safe to assume that relationships were essentially familial. . . .

What, essentially, held together this primordial human community? Was it the mutual usefulness to one another of those few hunters or fishers or farmers? To answer, "Yes," is to recognize what is obviously true: "Cooperation is essential to secure food and shelter and for defense against foes, human and subhuman." But to answer, "Yes," is also to suggest a possible misconception. The "identity of economic interests" of which Childe writes in the paragraph in which he so interestingly characterizes the mode of life of man before civilization, is a fact which any of us would have observed had we been there to see the precivilized community, and which is an obvious inference from what we know more directly about it. But this does not mean that in those communities men worked primarily for material wealth. The incentives to work and to exchange labor and goods are, in primitive and precivilized society especially, various and chiefly noneconomic (in the narrow sense). They arise from tradition, from a sense of obligation coming out of one's position in a system of status relationships, especially those of kinship, and from religious considerations and moral motivations of many kinds. . . .

To answer only that the precivilized community was held together by reason of mutual usefulness is to fail to say what it is that most importantly and characteristically holds such a community together. . . . It is the urban community that rests upon mutual usefulness. The primitive and precivilized communities are held together essentially by common understandings as to the ultimate nature and purpose of life. The precivilized society was like the present-day primitive society in those characteristics—isolation, smallness, homogeneity, persistence in the common effort to make a way of living under relatively stable circumstances—to which we have already attended, and therefore it was like the parallel societies which we can observe today in that its fundamental order was a matter of moral conviction. . . .

For the homogeneity of such a society is not that homogeneity in which everybody does the same thing at the same time. The people are homogeneous in that they share the same tradition and have the same view of the good life. They do the same kinds of work and they worship and marry and feel shame or pride in the same way and under similar circumstances. But at any one time the members of a primitive community may be doing notably different things: the women looking for edible roots while the men hunt; some men out on a war party while others at home perform a rite for its success. And when there is a familial ceremonial, or a magico-religious ritual affecting the whole community, the differences in what is being done may be very great. In the activities to gain a material living, labor, as between man and man or woman and woman, may be divided. But the total specialization of function, as among people of different sexes and age-or-kinship positions, and as among participants in a rite, may be very considerable. The point to be stressed is that all these activities conduce to a purpose, express a view of man's duty, that all share, and to which each activity or element of institution contributes.

We can safely say these things of the precivilized societies as we can say them of the primitive societies because these things follow from the other characteristics which we have already conceded, and are attested in every very isolated, undisturbed primitive society we observe today. . . .

The attempt to gather together some of the attributes of that form of human living which prevailed before the first civilizations arose may now be halted. . . . There results a picture, very generalized, of the organization of life, social control, and motivation among most of the societies of mankind during most of human history. The point upon which we are to insist, for its importance in considering the topics of the following lectures, is that in this early condition of humanity the essential order of society, the nexus which held people together, was moral. Humanity attained its characteristic, long-enduring nature as a multitude of different but equivalent systems of relationships and institutions each expressive of a view of the good. Each precivilized society was held together by largely undeclared but continually realized ethical conceptions. . . .

The antiquity of the moral order is not fully attested by archaeology. A people's conceptions as to the good are only meagerly represented in the material things that they make. A tribe of western Australia, the Pitjendadjara, today carry on a religious and moral life of great intensity, but they make and use material objects so few and so perishable that were these people exhibited to us only through archaeology, we would barely know that they had existed and we would know nothing of their moral life. As described by Charles P. Mountford in his charming book,[1] these aborigines perform their rites to increase animal and plant food, and they follow a morality of personal relations with dignity and conscience. Mountford says that they make but five tools: a spear, a spear-thrower, a wooden carrying dish, a stone slab on which to grind food, and a digging stick. Perhaps this investigator overlooked some of the articles made by these aborigines, but it is certainly true that naked and wandering, with almost none of the material possessions and power which we associate with the development of humanity, they are nevertheless as human as are you and I.

We may suppose that fifty thousand years ago mankind had developed a variety of moral orders, each expressed in some local tradition, and comparable to what we find among aborigines today. Their development required both the organic evolution of human bodily and cerebral nature and also the accumulation of experience by tradition. As the tradition began to accumulate while the organic evolution was still going on, the moral order—and the technical order—began to be established among the apelike men of the early Pleistocene. On the other hand, until bodily and cerebral nature

[1] Charles P. Mountford, *Brown Men and Red Sand* (Melbourne, Australia: Robertson E. Mullens, 1948).

equivalent to that of men living today had been developed, we cannot fairly attribute to those earliest humanoid societies a moral order comparable, let us say, with that of the Australian blackfellow. Even in the case of so relatively late a being as Neanderthal man there was a factor of biological difference which would have limited the development of culture. But by a time seventy-five or fifty thousand years ago, the biological evolution of mankind had reached a point at which the genetic qualities necessary for the development of fully human life had been attained. This reaches the conclusion that for a period of time at least five times as long as the entire period of civilization man has had the capacity for a life governed by such moral orders as we see in primitive societies today. The men who left the paintings of Altamira were fully human and not very different from us. And I follow Eliseo Vivas when he writes:

> That does not mean, of course, that they pursued the identical values and were capable of the same theoretical sophistication of which we are capable; it merely means that they probably had the same degree of moral sensibility, though perhaps focused toward different objects than those toward which we, the men of contemporary technological society, focus ours.[2]

In recognizing that every precivilized society of the past fifty or seventy-five millenniums had a moral order to which the technical order was subordinate, I do not say that the religious and ethical systems of these societies were equally complex. Then, as now, there were "thin cultures" and "rich cultures." Childe sees certain of the Mesolithic cultures as "thin" in comparison with the cultures that preceded them. It is not, of course, clear that the thinness lay in the moral life. Maybe they had a religious and personal life that is not represented in the archaeology. However this may be in that particular case, we are to recognize that the development of technology had, even in precivilized times, an important influence on the moral life. While the Australians show us how little material culture is needed for the development of a moral order, such a contrast as that between the Haida and the Paiute Indians reminds us that generally speaking a people desperately concerned with getting a living cannot develop a rich moral or esthetic life. The moral order of a hard-pressed people may be itself simple. But I insist that it is there in every case. . . .

We may conceive of the moral order as equally present in those

⁎ Eliseo Vivas, *The Moral Life and the Ethical Life* (Chicago: University of Chicago Press, 1950), p. 105.

societies in which the rules for right conduct among men are supported by supernatural sanctions and in those in which the morality of human conduct is largely independent of the religion (in the sense of belief and cult about the supernatural). "Moral order" includes the binding sentiments of rightness that attend religion, the social solidarity that accompanies religious ritual, the sense of religious seriousness and obligation that strengthens men, and the effects of a belief in invisible beings that embody goodness. The moral order becomes vivid to us when we think of the Australian Arunta assembling, each man to do his part, denying himself food, making the sacred marks or performing the holy dances, that the witchetty-grub may become numerous and the whole band thus continue to find its food. Or of the old Chinese family performing the rituals for the ancestors. Or of the members of the boys' gang refusing, even in the face of threats from the police, to "tell on" a fellow member.

By a corresponding extension of another and more familiar term, all the other forms of coordination of activity which appear in human societies may be brought together and contrasted with the moral order under the phrase "the technical order." The bonds that coordinate the activities of men in the technical order do not rest on convictions as to the good life; they are not characterized by a foundation in human sentiments; they can exist even without the knowledge of those bound together that they are bound together. The technical order is that order which results from mutual usefulness, from deliberate coercion, or from the mere utilization of the same means. In the technical order men are bound by things, or are themselves things. They are organized by necessity or expediency. Think, if you will, of the orderly way in which automobiles move in response to the traffic light or the policeman's whistle, or think of the flow of goods, services, and money among the people who together produce, distribute, and consume some commodity such as rubber.

Civilization may be thought of as the antithesis of the folk society. It may also, and consistently with the first antithesis, be thought of as that society in which the relations between technical order and moral order take forms radically different from the relationships between the two which prevail in precivilized society.

Civilization (conceived now as one single thing and not—as by Toynbee—as twenty-one different things) may be said to exist to the extent, to the degree, and in the respects in which a society has developed away from the kind of precivilized society which I have been describing. Civilization is, of course, things added to society: cities, writing, public works, the state, the market, and so forth. Another way of looking at it is from the base provided by the folk society. Then we may say that a society is civilized insofar as the community is no longer small, isolated, homogeneous and self-sufficient; as the division of labor is no longer simple; as impersonal relationships come to take the place of personal relationships; as familial connections come to be modified or supplanted by those of political affiliation or contract; and as thinking has become reflective and systematic. I do not mention all of the characteristics of folk societies which I named in foregoing paragraphs; these are enough to suggest the point of view we might adopt. If we do adopt this way of conceiving civilization, we shall think of Toynbee's twenty-one civilizations as different developments away from the folk society. We see then that civilizations do not depart from the nature of the folk society evenly or in the same way. In Chinese civilization the organization of social relationships according to the categories and attitudes of kinship retained its importance while philosophy and the fine arts passed through long histories of development. The Andean civilization developed political and administrative institutions of impressive complexity and far-reaching influence while yet the Indians who developed them were without writing. The Mayan peoples, in contrast, extended their political institutions little beyond that attained by the ordinary tribe while their intellectual specialists carried some parts of mathematics and astronomy to heights that astonish us. In short, the several civilizations start up from their folk bases into specialized development in which some elements of the folk society are left behind while others are retained. Yet this fact does not destroy the impression that, as a manner of life taken as a whole, civilization is one kind of thing different from the life of the folk society.

The contrast between technical order and moral order helps us to understand the general kind of thing which is civilization. In the folk society the moral order is great and the technical order is small. In primitive and precivilized societies material tools are few and little natural power is used. Neither the formal regulations of the state or church nor the nonmoral ordering of behavior which occurs in the market plays an important part in these societies. It is civilization that develops them.

It is civilization, too, that develops those formal and apparent institutions which both express the moral order and are means toward its realization. The technical order appears not only in tools,

power, and an interdependence of people chiefly or wholly impersonal and utilitarian, but also in greater and more varied apparatus
for living—apparatus both physical and institutional. Under ten
headings Childe[3] has summarized the characteristics of civilized life
whether lived at Uruk, Mohenjo-daro, or Uxmal among the
Mayans. One, the reappearance of naturalistic art, has a significance
not immediately plain, and may be a little doubtful. Of the other
nine, six plainly announce the growth of the technical order: (1)
the great increase in the size of the settlement (the material equipment for human association becomes far larger); (2) the institution
of tribute or taxation with resulting central accumulation of capital;
(3) monumental public works; (4) the art of writing; (5) the
beginnings of such exact and predictive sciences as arithmetic,
geometry, and astronomy; and (6) developed economic institutions
making possible a greatly expanded foreign trade. Each of these six
suggests the increasing complexity of social organization, and the
remaining three criteria explicitly declare features of that social
organization which are characteristic of civilization; (7) full-time
technical specialists, as in metal-working; (8) a privileged ruling
class; and (9) the state, or the organization of society on a basis of
residence in place of, or on top of, a basis of kinship.

In folk societies the moral order predominates over the technical
order. It is not possible, however, simply to reverse this statement
and declare that in civilizations the technical order predominates
over the moral. In civilization the technical order certainly becomes
great. But we cannot truthfully say that in civilization the moral
order becomes small. There are ways in civilization in which the
moral order takes on new greatness. In civilization the relations
between the two orders are varying and complex.

The great transformations of humanity are only in part reported
in terms of the revolutions in technology with resulting increases in
the number of people living together. There have also occurred
changes in the thinking and valuing of men which may also be
called "radical and indeed revolutionary innovations." Like
changes in the technical order, these changes in the intellectual and
moral habits of men become themselves generative of far-reaching
changes in the nature of human living. They do not reveal themselves in events as visible and particular as do material inventions,
or even always as increasing complexity in the systems of social relationships. Nor is it perhaps possible to associate the moral trans-

[3] V. G. Childe, "The Urban Revolution," *Town Planning Review*, XXI (1950),
3-17.

formations with limited periods of time as we can associate technological revolutions with particular spans of years. Yet the attempt to identify some of the transformations in men's minds can be made.

One might begin such an attempt by examining the manner of life of the most primitive people we know today, and perhaps also something that is told us about ancient peoples, for evidence of the appearance of forms of thought, belief, or action which a little knowledge of the history of some civilization shows us became influential in changing human life. We see some far-reaching change in the moral or intellectual life of the Western world, perhaps, and so guided we return to the primitive societies to see if it had a beginning there. So we might come to some understanding of some of the relations in history between the two kinds of orders.

As to the trend of this relationship throughout history, I have one general impression. It is that the moral order begins as something pre-eminent but incapable of changing itself, and becomes perhaps less eminent but more independent. In folk society the moral rules bend, but men cannot make them afresh. In civilization the old moral orders suffer, but new states of mind are developed by which the moral order is, to some significant degree, taken in charge. The story of the moral order is attainment of some autonomy through much adversity.

FURTHER READINGS

The following works are recommended as suitable for the student or layman. Titles marked with an asterisk are available in paperback editions.

General

Boule, M., and H. Vallois, *Fossil Men*. New York: The Dryden Press, Inc., 1957. The most comprehensive book on fossil man. Somewhat out-of-date but useful as a reference text.

*Braidwood, R. J., *Prehistoric Men*, Chicago Natural History Museum, Popular Series, No. 37, 1957. A brief and simplified description of cultural development from earliest times until the rise of civilization. Emphasis on the Near East in those sections dealing with later prehistory.

————, and G. Willey, eds., *Courses toward Urban Life*. Viking Fund Publication, No. 32, Wenner-Gren Foundation for Anthropological Research, Inc., 1962. A more technical volume consisting of essays by specialists on the prehistoric archaeology of most major areas in the world. Primary intent is to explain why civilizations arose in some areas while alternative developments occurred elsewhere.

*Childe, V. G., *Man Makes Himself*. London: Watts & Co., 1948. A general survey of man's achievements, with the original definitions by Childe of the Neolithic and Urban Revolutions.

*————, *What Happened in History*. Harmondsworth, England: Penguin Books, 1946. Human history from Paleolithic times until the decline and fall of the ancient civilizations.

*Clark, J. G. D., *Archaeology and Society*. Cambridge, Mass.: Harvard University Press, 1957. An excellent example of what the archaeologist attempts to learn of human society from prehistoric cultural remains.

*————, *World Prehistory: An Outline*. Cambridge, England: Cambridge University Press, 1961. One of the few books attempting to present prehistory on a world-wide scale. Reasonably authoritative but less satisfactory for the Americas than for the Old World.

Clark, Sir Wilfred Le Gros, *The Fossil Evidence for Human Evolution.* Chicago: University of Chicago Press, 1955. An expert presents his views of how to interpret the fossil remains of early man and a broad reconstruction of human evolution.

Hawkes, J., and Sir Leonard Woolley, *Prehistory and the Beginnings of Civilization.* New York: Harper & Row, Publishers, 1963. The first volume of the UNESCO series on world history. A very good account of prehistoric life and early civilization, with excellent illustrations.

Heizer, R. F., ed., *The Archaeologist at Work.* New York: Harper & Row, Publishers, 1959. A collection of short essays showing how archaeologists interpret their finds.

*————, *Man's Discovery of His Past.* Englewood Cliffs, N.J.: Prentice-Hall, Inc., 1962. Original accounts of great discoveries in archaeology, with a bibliography of other works relating to the history of the field.

Lasker, G. W., *The Evolution of Man.* New York: Holt, Rinehart & Winston, Inc., 1961. A short introduction to physical anthropology, with emphasis on human evolution.

*Leakey, L. S. B., *Adam's Ancestors.* New York: Harper & Row, Publishers, 1960. The evolution of man and development of culture during the Paleolithic.

*Montagu, M. F. A., *Culture and the Evolution of Man.* New York: Oxford University Press, 1962. Essays on the relationships of culture, biology, and environment that illustrate current trends in research on early man.

*Oakley, K. P., *Man the Tool-Maker.* British Museum (Natural History), 1956. An introductory text on Paleolithic technology, describing types of stone tools and how they were made.

Zeuner, F. E., *Dating the Past.* London: Methuen & Co., Ltd., 1958. The standard text on dating methods for students of archaeology.

Africa

Alimen, H., *The Prehistory of Africa.* London: Hutchinson & Co. (Publishers), 1957. The only book in English covering the archaeology of the whole African continent. Deals mostly with technology and Pleistocene geology.

These three volumes constitute the best introduction to African archaeology.

*Clark, J. D., *The Prehistory of Southern Africa.* Harmondsworth, England: Penguin Books, 1959.

*Cole, S., *The Prehistory of East Africa.* Harmondsworth, England: Penguin Books, 1954 (rev. ed., The Macmillan Co., 1963).

* McBurney, C. B. M., *The Stone Age of Northern Africa.* Harmondsworth, England: Penguin Books, 1960.

Europe and the Near East

*Burkitt, M. C., *The Old Stone Age.* London: Bowes & Bowes, Publishers, Ltd., 1955. A standard text on Lower and Upper Paleolithic archaeology.

*Childe, V. G., *New Light on the Most Ancient East.* London: Routledge & Kegan Paul, Ltd., 1952. A comprehensive description of early civilizations in southwest Asia, Egypt, and the Indus and of their prehistoric foundations.

*———, *The Prehistory of European Society.* Harmondsworth, England: Penguin Books, 1958. A broad account of prehistoric archaeology in Europe, with emphasis placed on the Neolithic and the Bronze Age.

Clark, J. G. D., *Prehistoric Europe: The Economic Basis.* Cambridge, England: Cambridge University Press, 1952. The best descriptive interpretation of prehistoric technology and economy from Upper Paleolithic to Iron Age times. Illustrates good use of comparative ethnographic material for archaeological interpretation.

*Frankfort, H., *The Birth of Civilization in the Near East.* Bloomington, Ind.: Indiana University Press, 1951. A good account of Egyptian and southwest Asian archaeology.

*Wilson, J., *The Culture of Ancient Egypt.* Chicago: University of Chicago Press, 1956. An introduction to the study of early civilization in the Nile Valley. Originally published as *The Burden of Egypt.*

The Far East

Chêng, Tê-k'un, *Archaeology in China, I: Prehistoric China.* Cambridge, England: W. Heffer & Sons, Ltd., 1959. This work, with subsequent volumes on later periods, is probably the most comprehensive account of archaeology in China.

*Fairservis, W. A., Jr., *The Origins of Oriental Civilization.* New York: Mentor Books, 1959. A general treatment of Far Eastern archaeology. Covers the whole span of prehistory from Paleolithic times up through the rise of civilization in China and Japan.

Kidder, J. E., *Japan before Buddhism.* London: Thames & Hudson, 1959. The most reliable account of Japanese prehistory in English.

Li Chi, *The Beginnings of Chinese Civilization.* Seattle, Wash.: University of Washington Press, 1957. A brief presentation, based on a lecture series, of Chinese archaeology.

*Piggott, S., *Prehistoric India*. Harmondsworth, England: Penguin Books, 1950. A useful introduction to the prehistory of the Indus Valley.

Watson, W., *China before the Han Dynasty*. London: Thames & Hudson, 1961. A good introduction to Chinese archaeology.

Wheeler, Sir Mortimer, *Early India and Pakistan*. London: Thames & Hudson, 1959. The best introduction to the archaeology of the Indian subcontinent.

The Americas

*Bushnell, G. H. S., *Peru*. London: Thames & Hudson, 1963. Broad coverage of Andean archaeology.

Coe, M. D., *Mexico*. London: Thames & Hudson, 1962. The archaeology of pre-Columbian Mexico.

Griffin, J. B., *Archeology of Eastern United States*. Chicago: University of Chicago Press, 1952. A collection of essays on the archaeology of different parts of the eastern United States. Some of the selections are out-of-date.

Martin, P., G. Quimby, and D. Collier, *Indians before Columbus*. Chicago: University of Chicago Press, 1947. A handbook of prehistoric peoples in the United States and the Arctic. Considerably out-of-date.

*Mason, J. A., *Ancient Civilization of Peru*. Harmondsworth, England: Penguin Books, 1957. Prehistoric cultures of the Andes, with a good description of the Incas.

Morley, S. G., *The Ancient Maya,* rev. by G. W. Brainerd. Stanford University Press, 1954. A thorough introduction to the ancient Mayas and their accomplishments.

Thompson, J. E., *The Rise and Fall of Maya Civilization*. Norman, Okla.: Oklahoma University Press, 1954. A good description of Mayan civilization for the layman.

*Vaillant, G., *The Aztecs of Mexico*. Harmondsworth, England: Penguin Books, 1950. Life and times of the Aztecs, with chapters on their prehistoric predecessors.

*Willey, G., and P. Phillips, *Method and Theory in American Archaeology*. Chicago: University of Chicago Press, 1958. An attempt to synthesize the prehistoric cultures of the entire Western Hemisphere.

*Wormington, H. M., *Ancient Man in North America*. Denver Museum of Natural History, Popular Series, No. 4, 1957. The best general coverage of early man in the New World.